Thank You!

Thank you for making a choice to include a Kapito Coloring Book in your life! With so many choices out there in the world, it makes our hearts swell with joy whenever someone like you chooses a Kapito book.

Let us know how we did!

Please give this book an honest review on Amazon, and let us know your experience. It's truly appreciated, and helps us to improve over time. If you enjoyed coloring this book, it's always a pleasure to know we gave you a positive experience.

About Kapito Coloring Books

The world is a constantly changing place, and grows increasingly complex. We believe that it's important to take some time to yourself, to do something creative and simple, to center your focus and find your inner joys. There is no such thing as a wrong way to color a Kapito Coloring Book, so let your creative juices flow, and follow your heart. Our books are designed with a watermark on the flip side of each image, so you can feel free to use crayons, markers, colored pencils and even paints.

Follow or Friend Us on Social Media

A Product of Kapito Coloring Books
www.kapitocoloringbooks.com

Have a question? Contact us!
kapitocoloringbooks@gmail.com

Copyright 2023, Kapito Coloring Books, All Rights Reserved

No part of this coloring book may be reproduced or transmitted in any format or by any means, whether electronic or mechanical, or via photocopying, without the written permission of Kapito Coloring Books, except in the case of media reviews of our works.

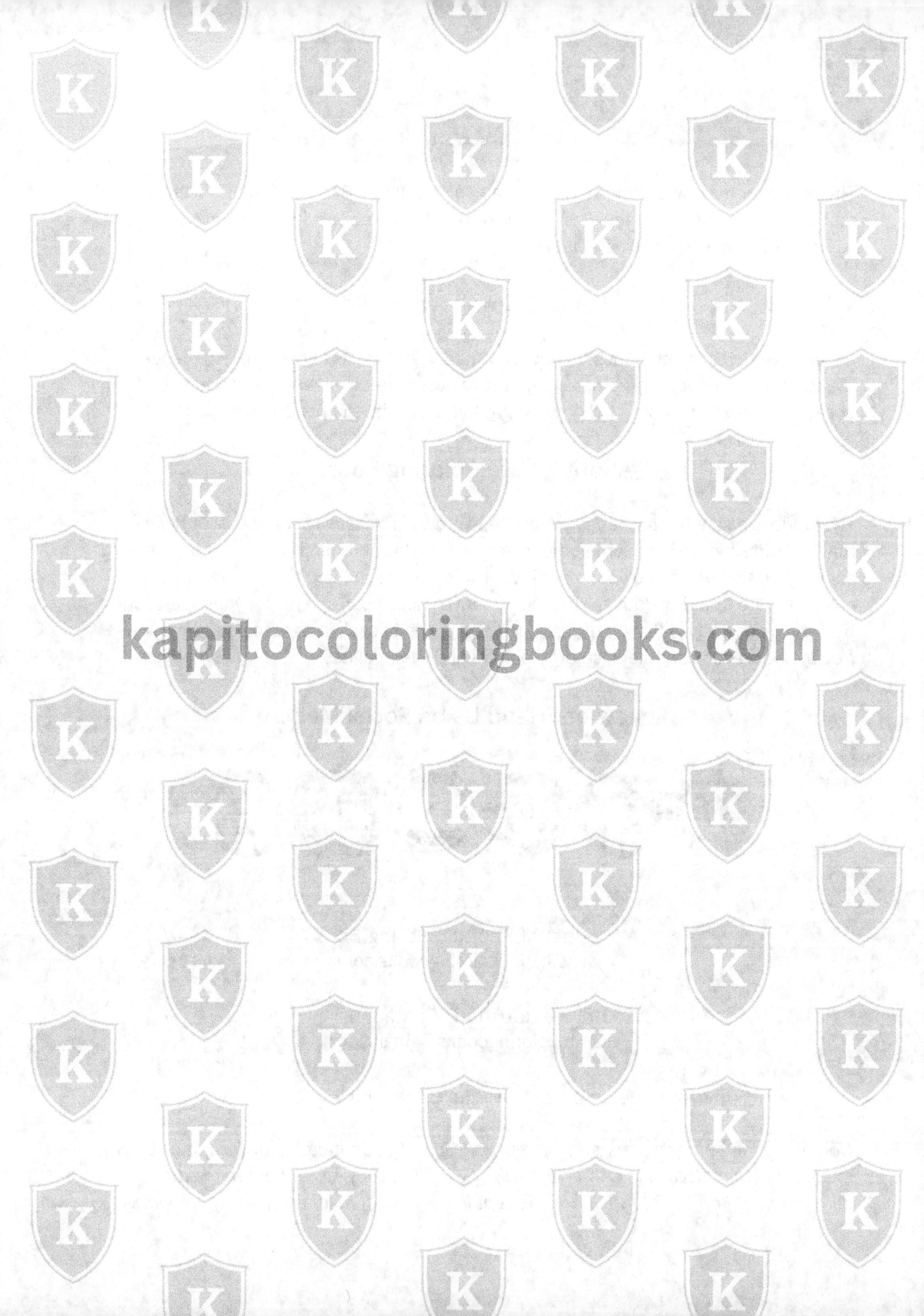

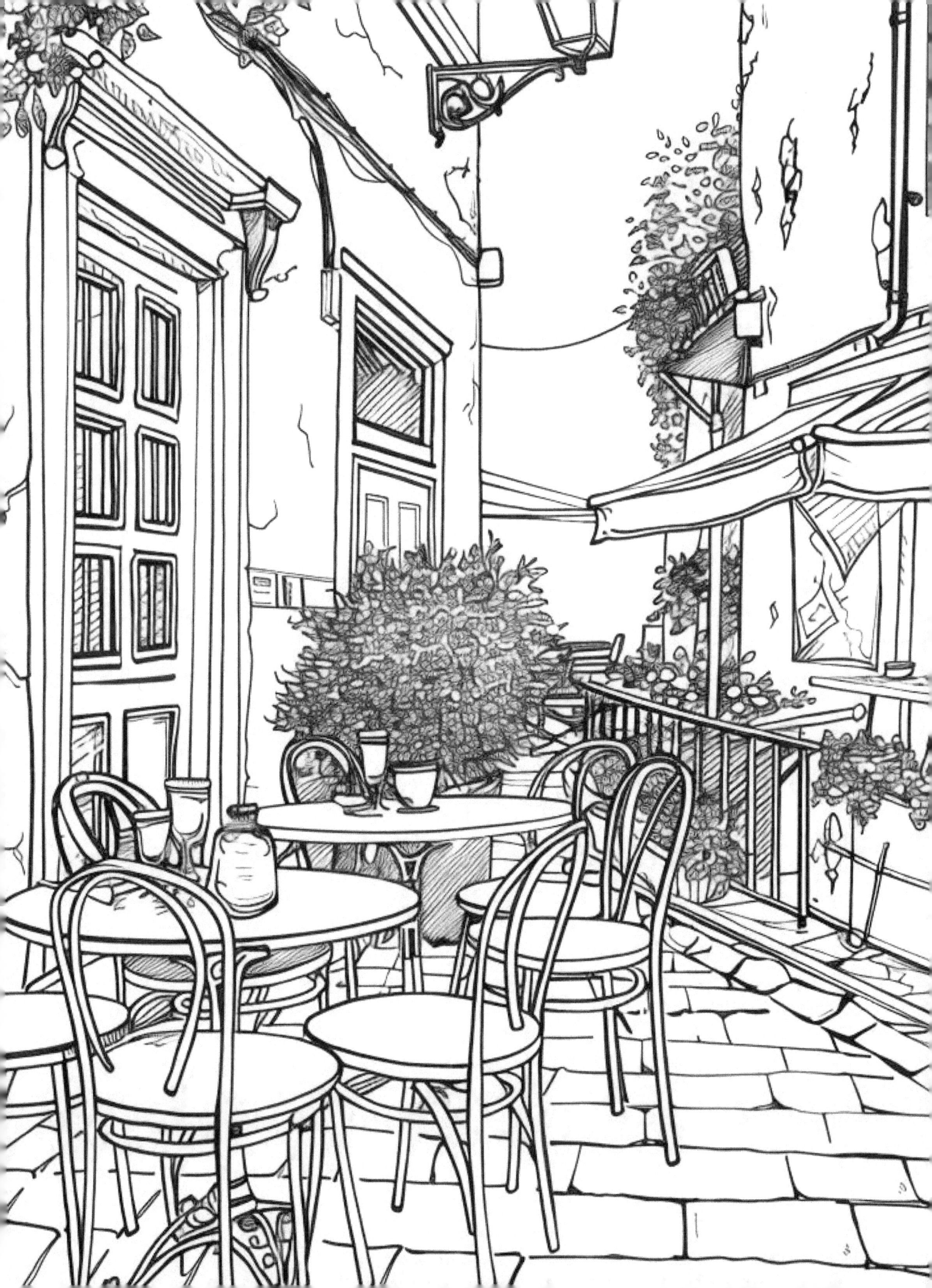

kapitocoloringbooks.com

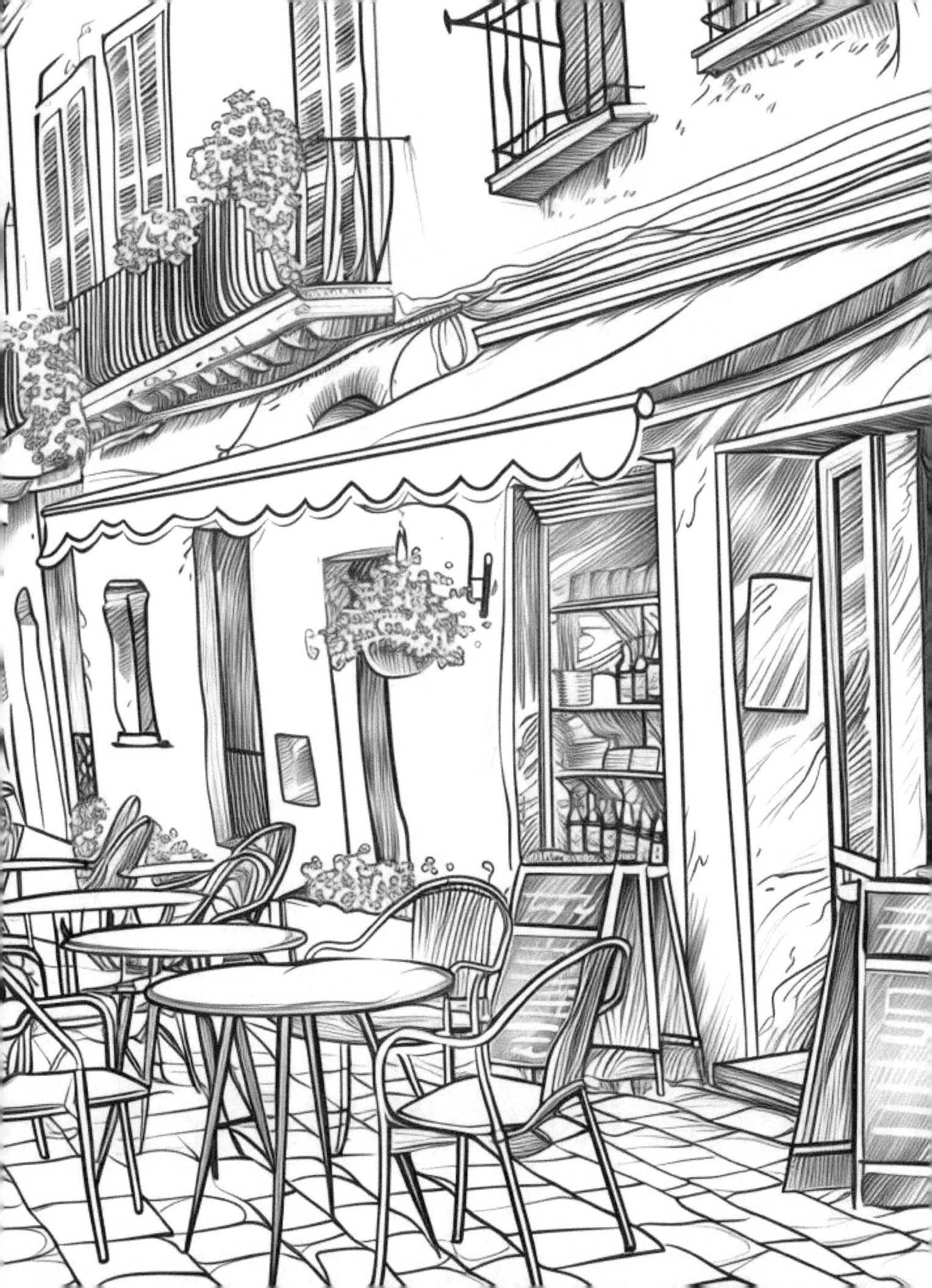

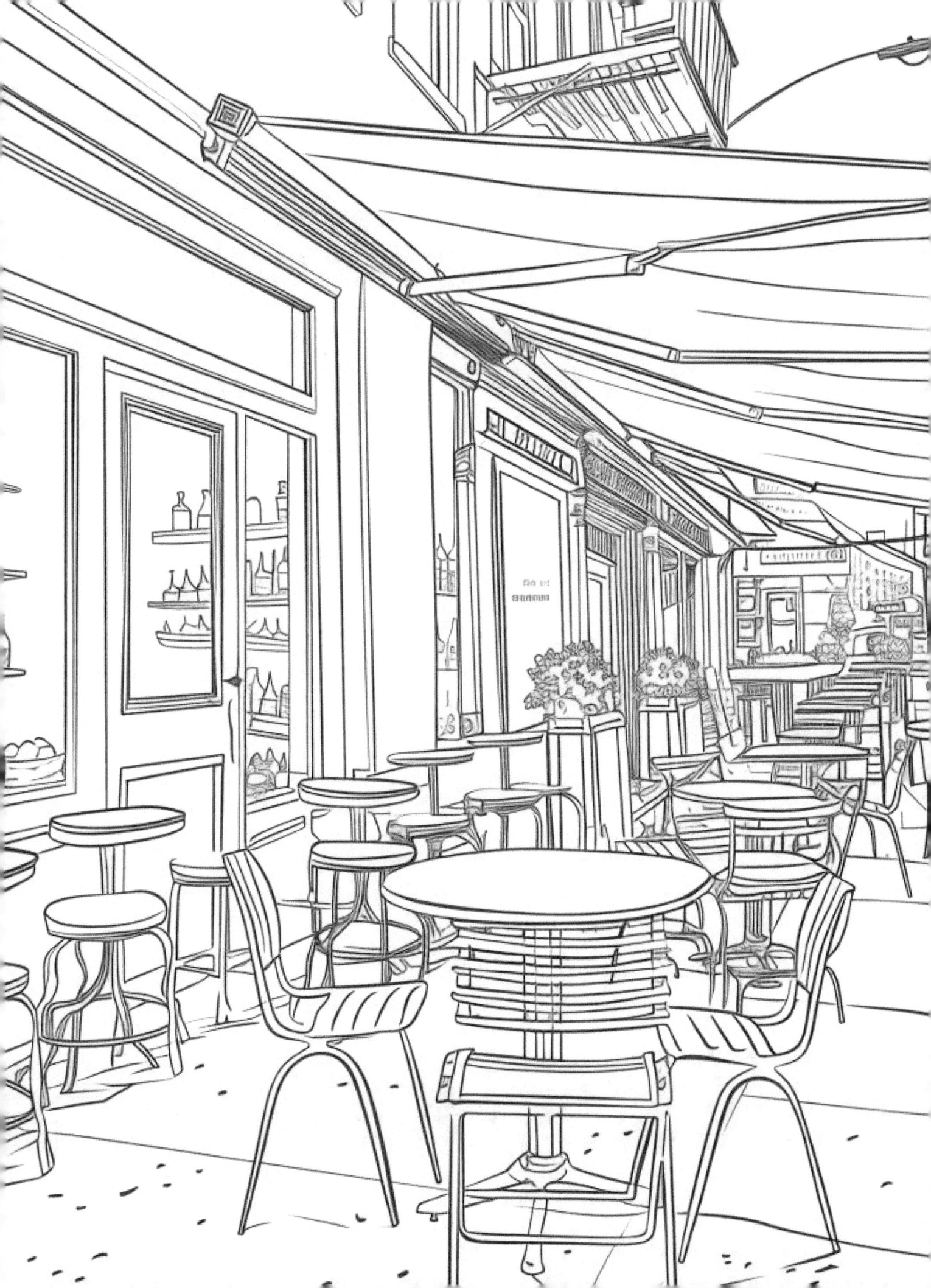

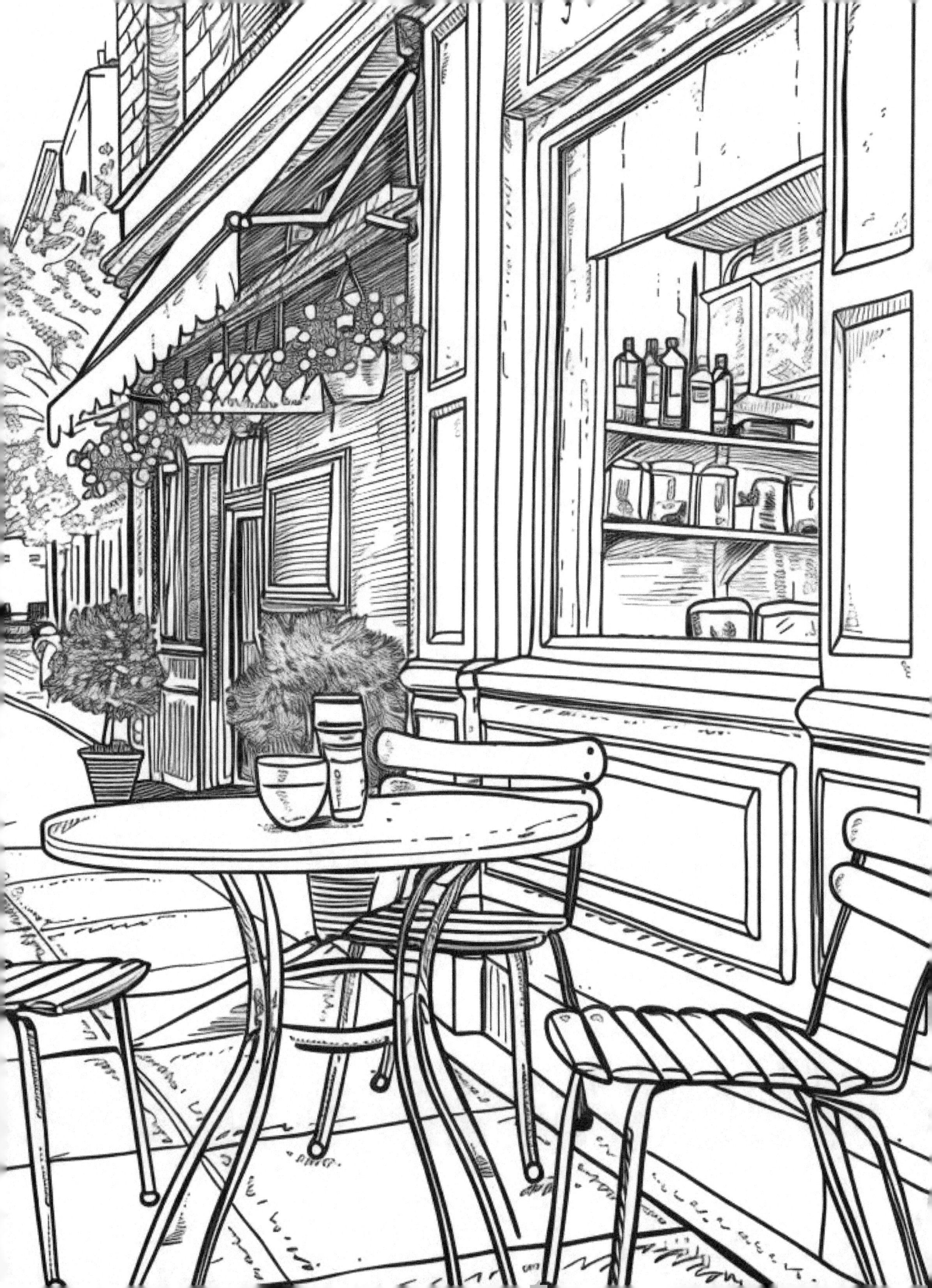

kapitocoloringbooks.com

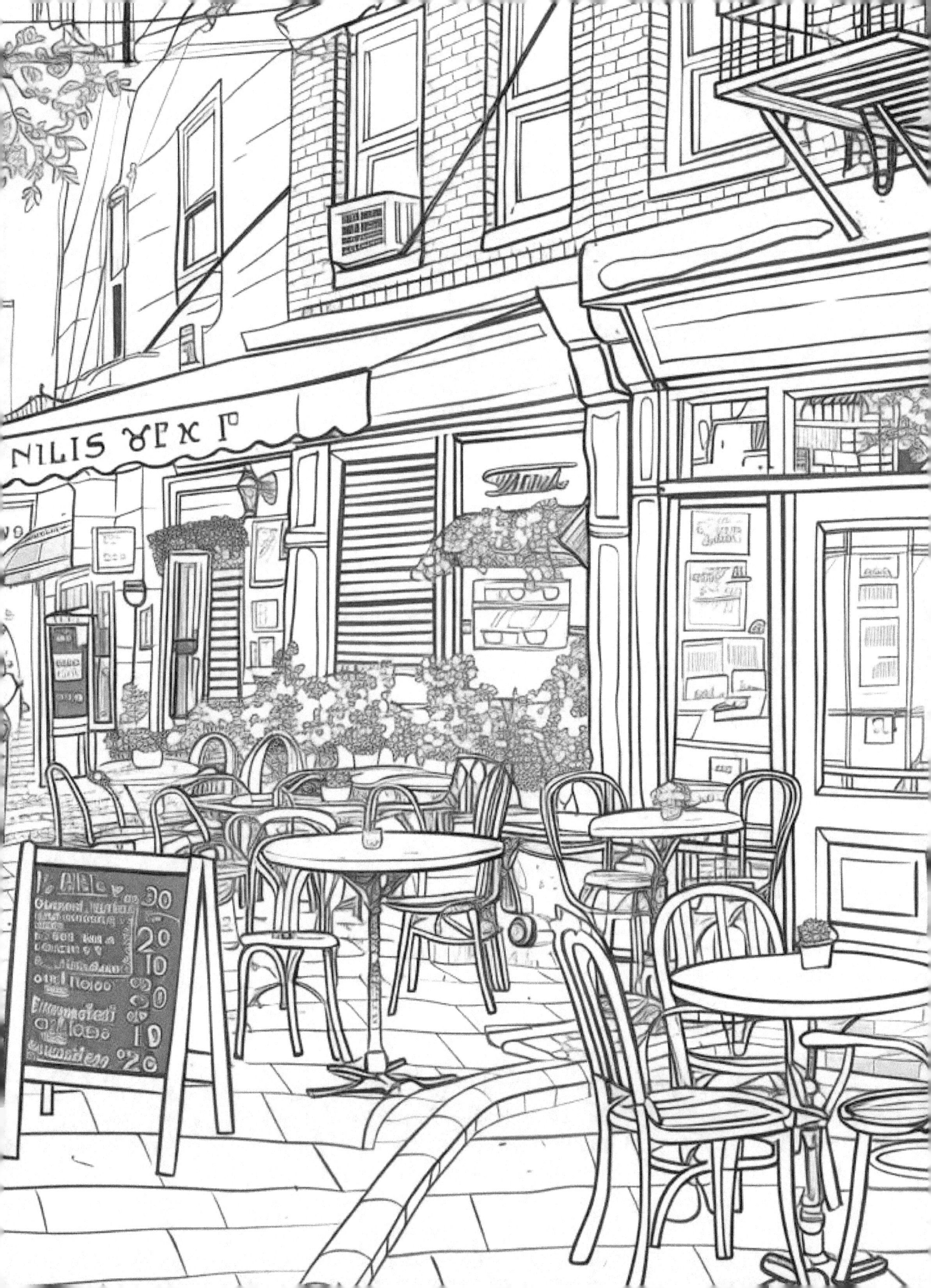

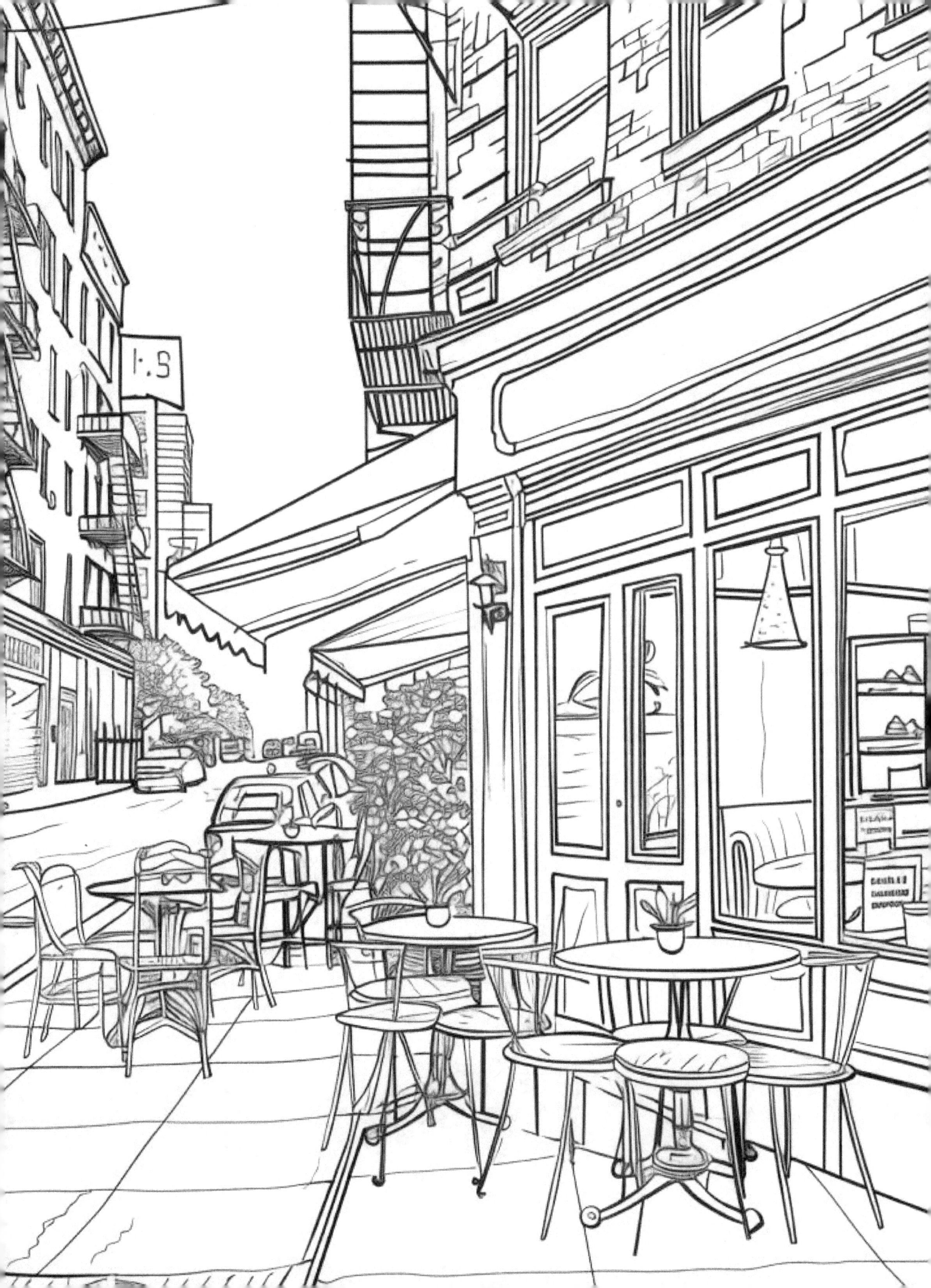

kapitocoloringbooks.com

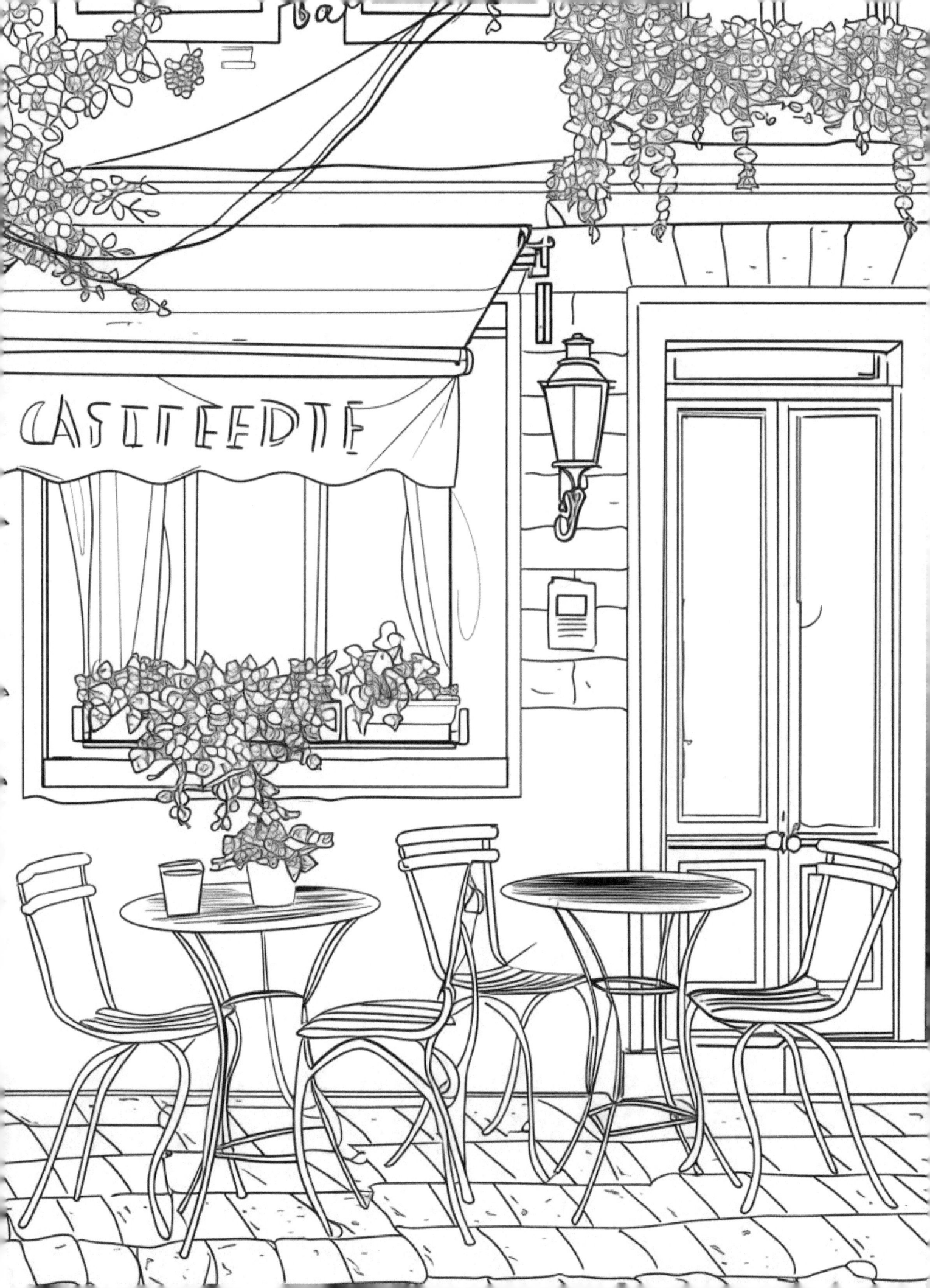

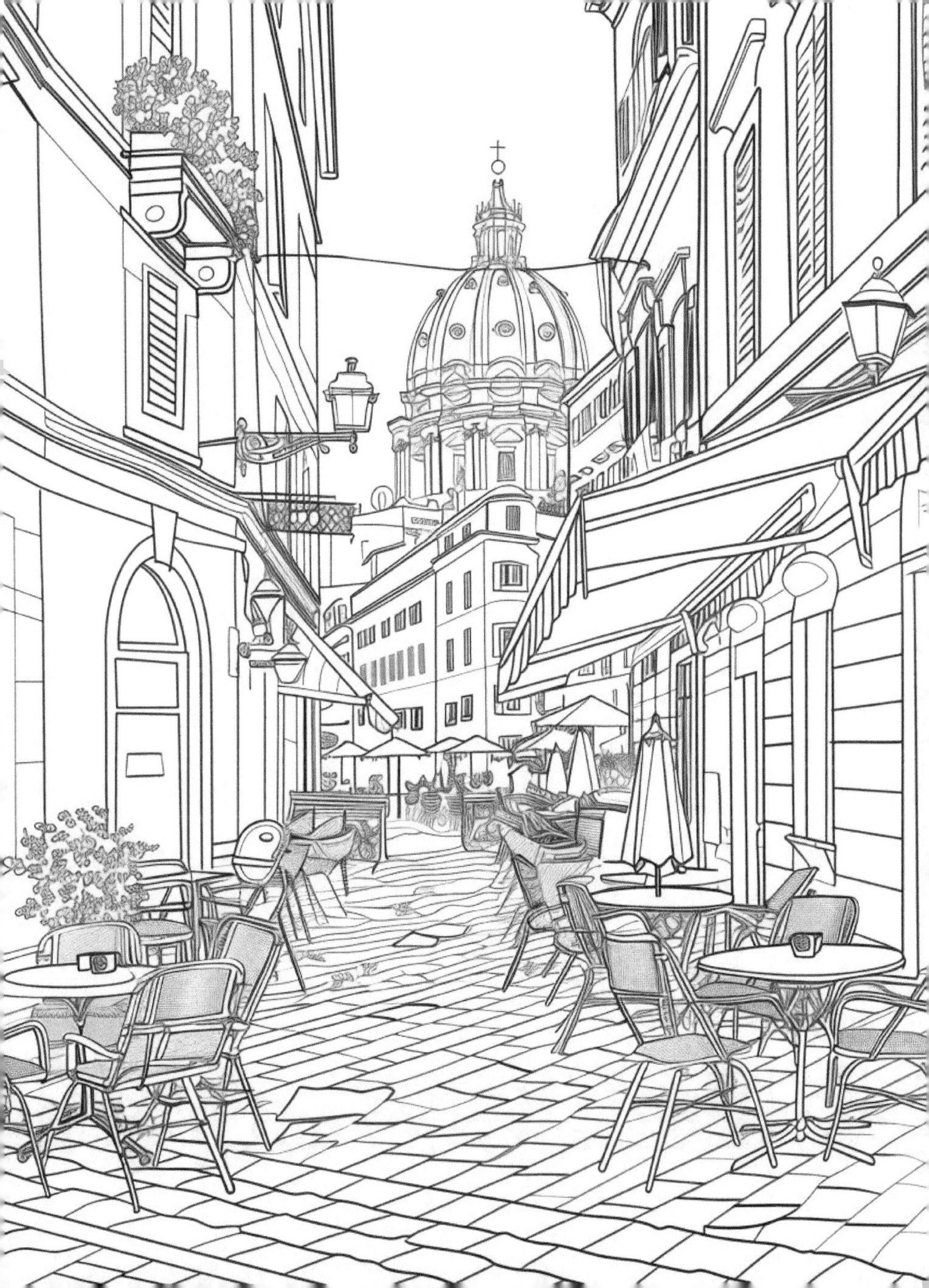

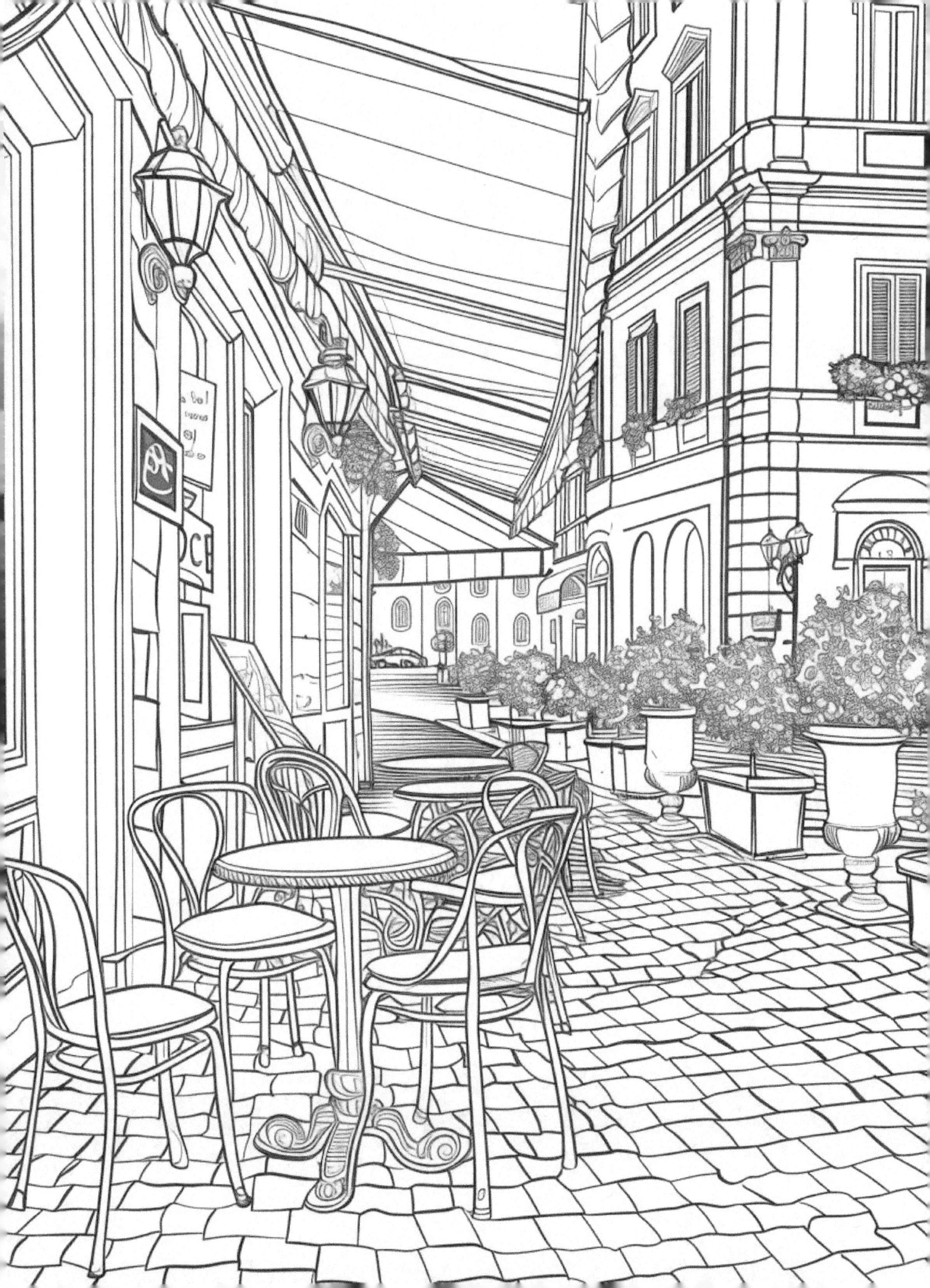

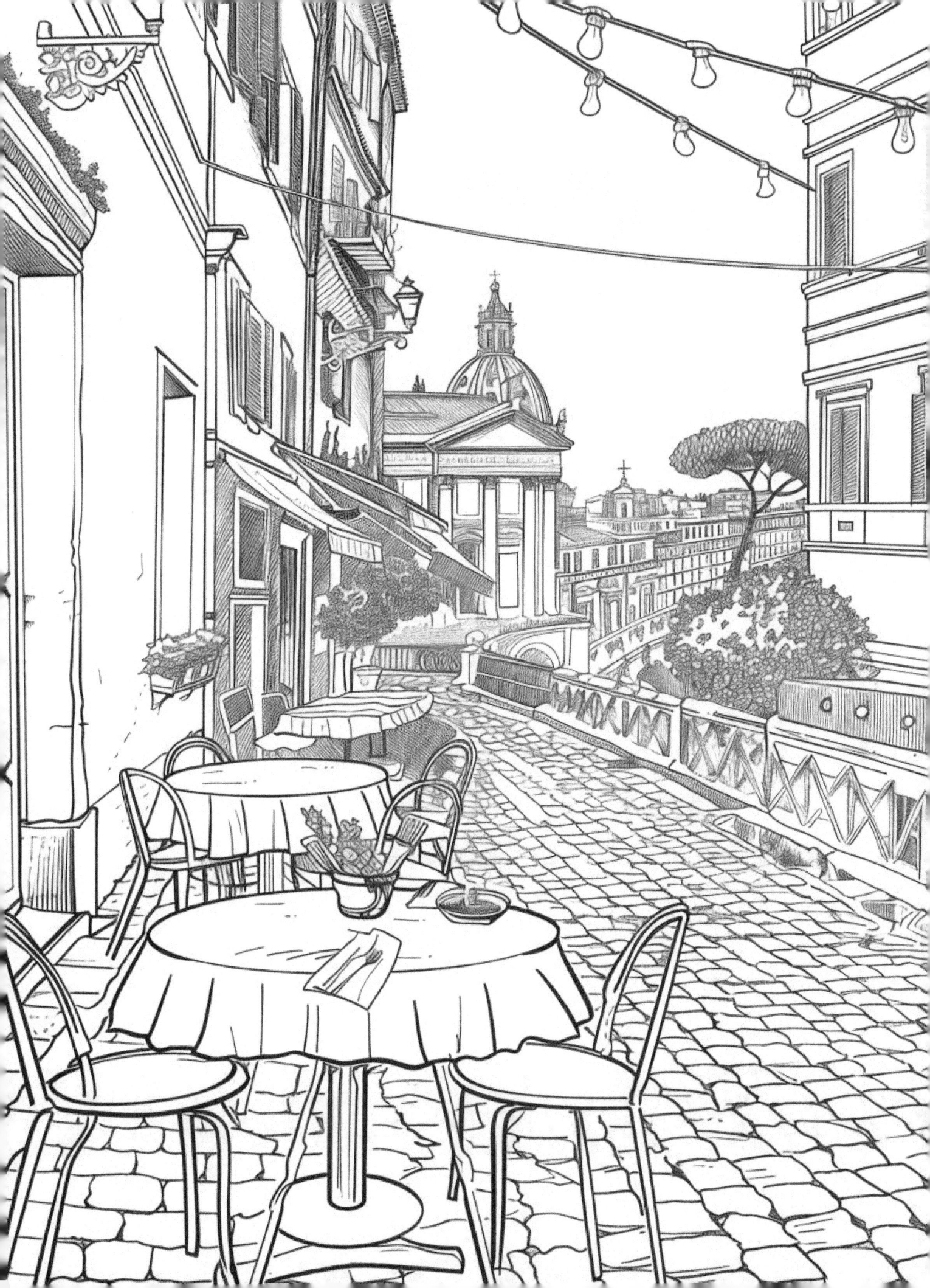

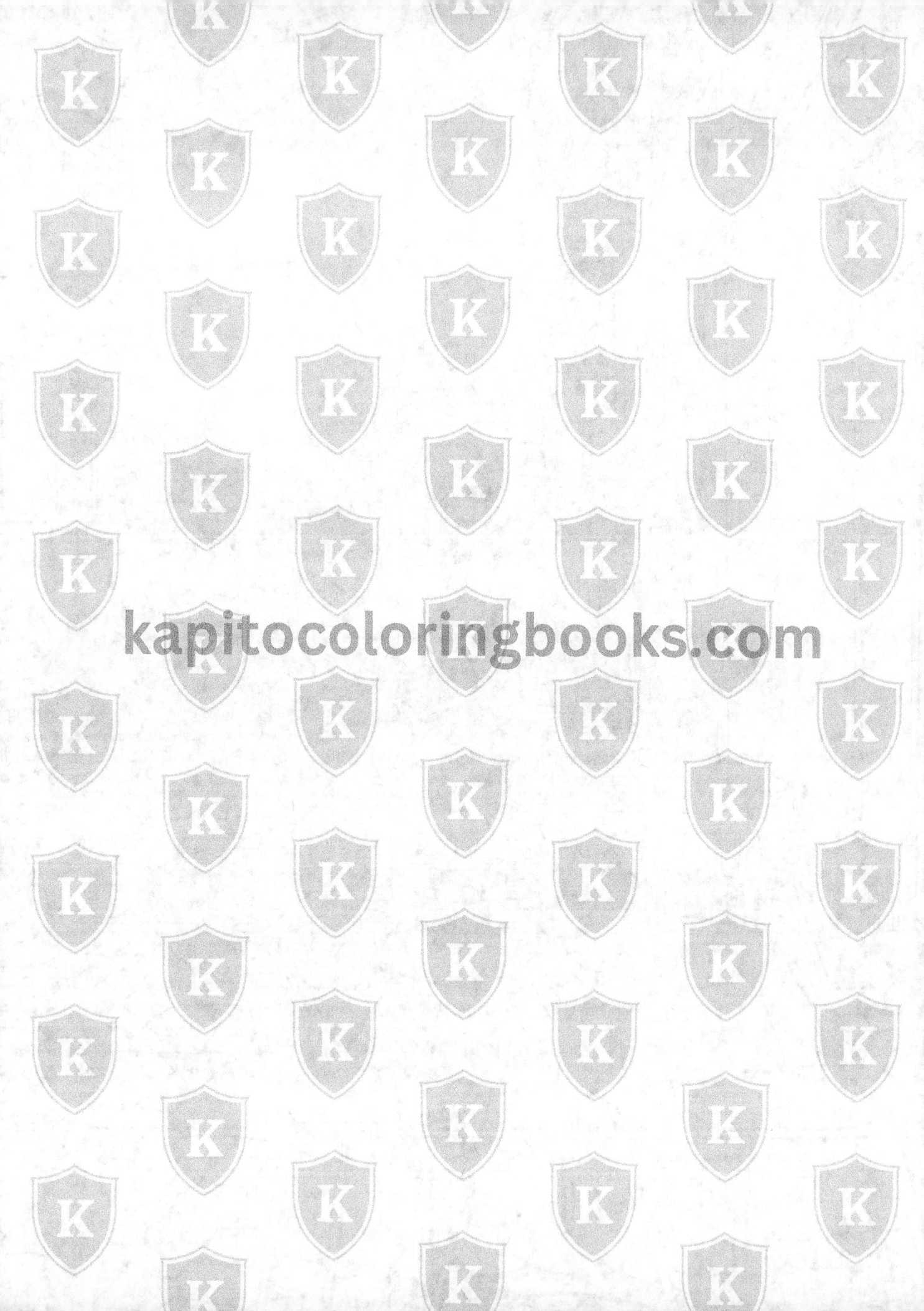

kapitocoloringbooks.com

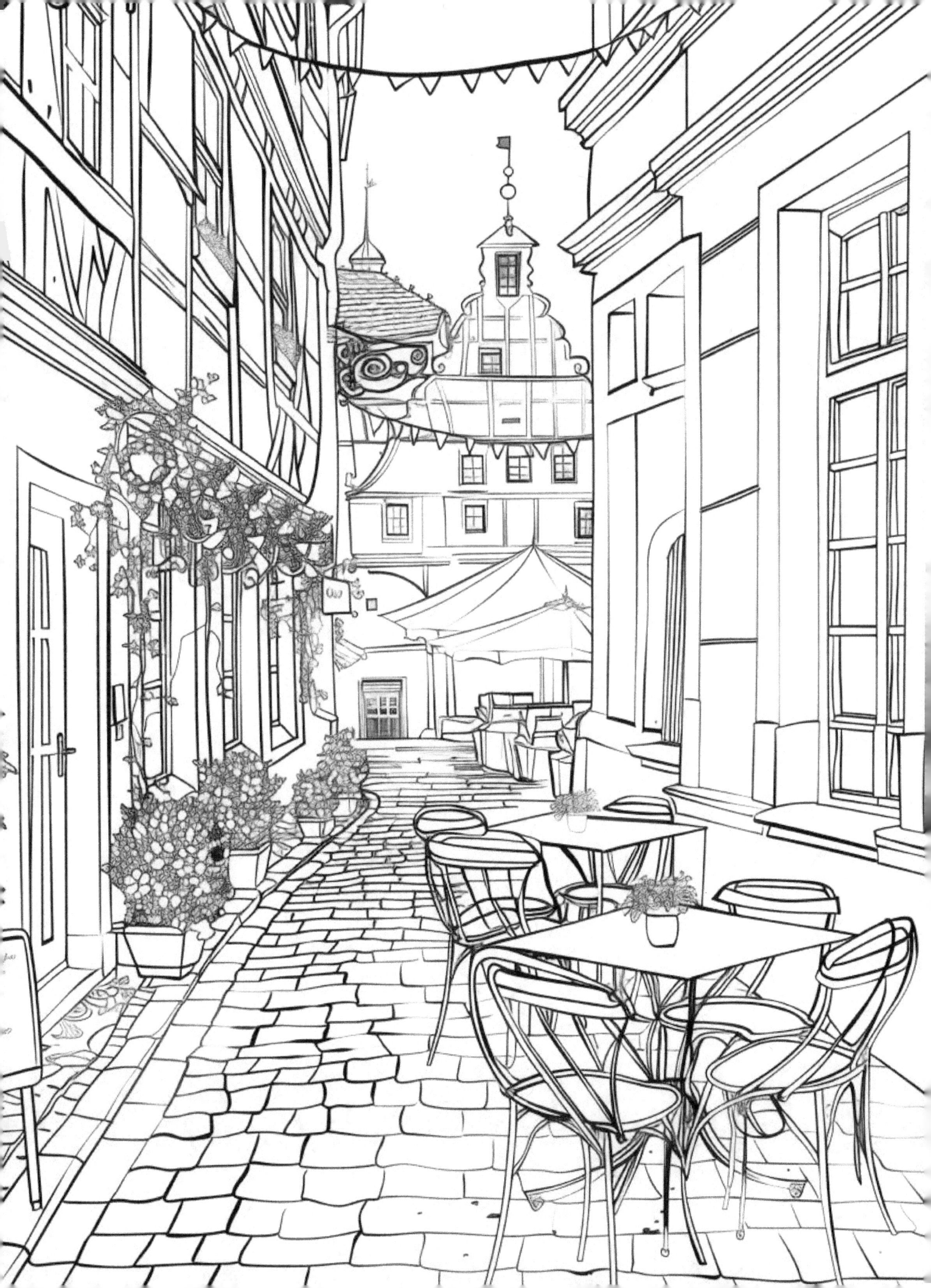

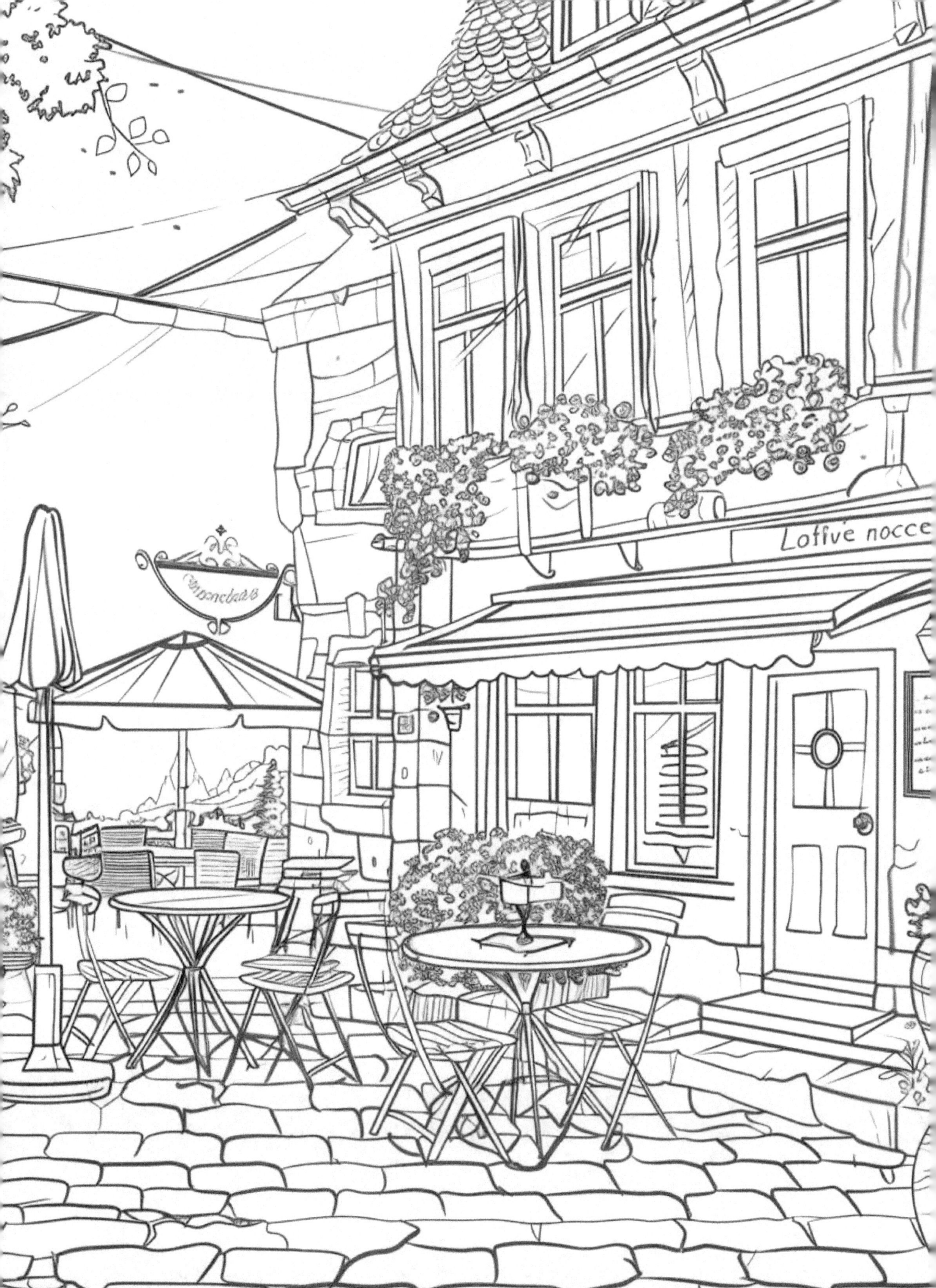

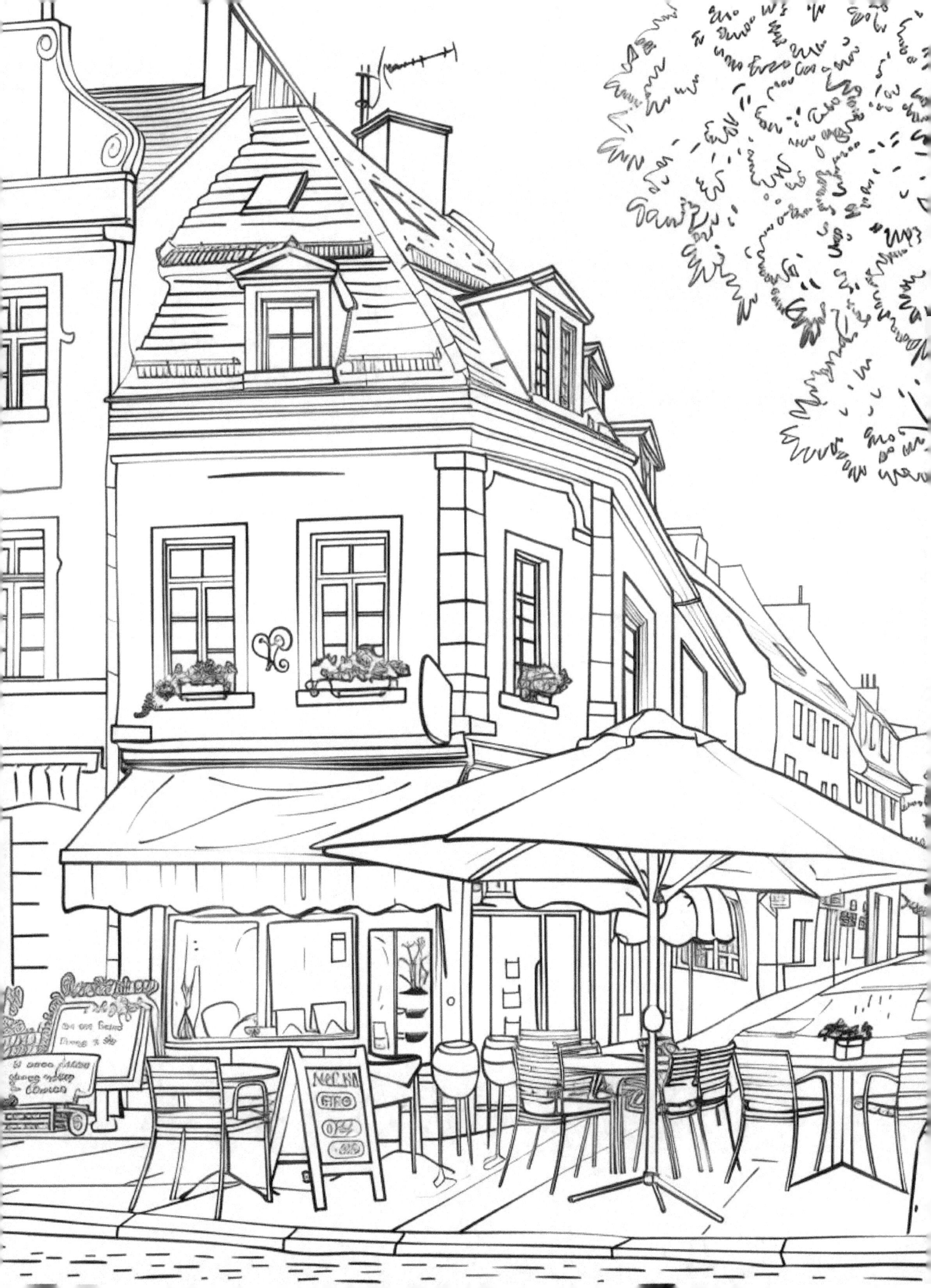

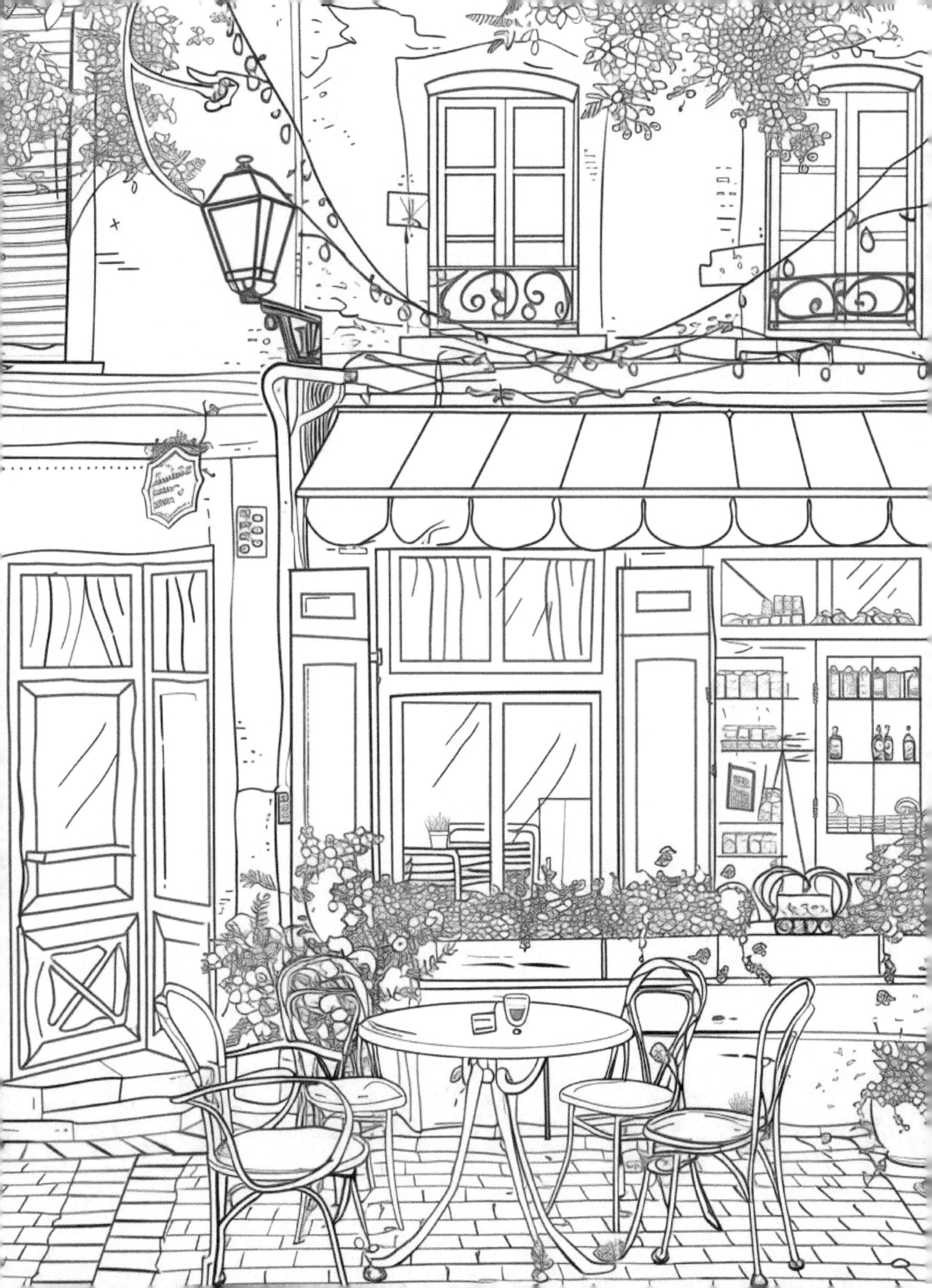

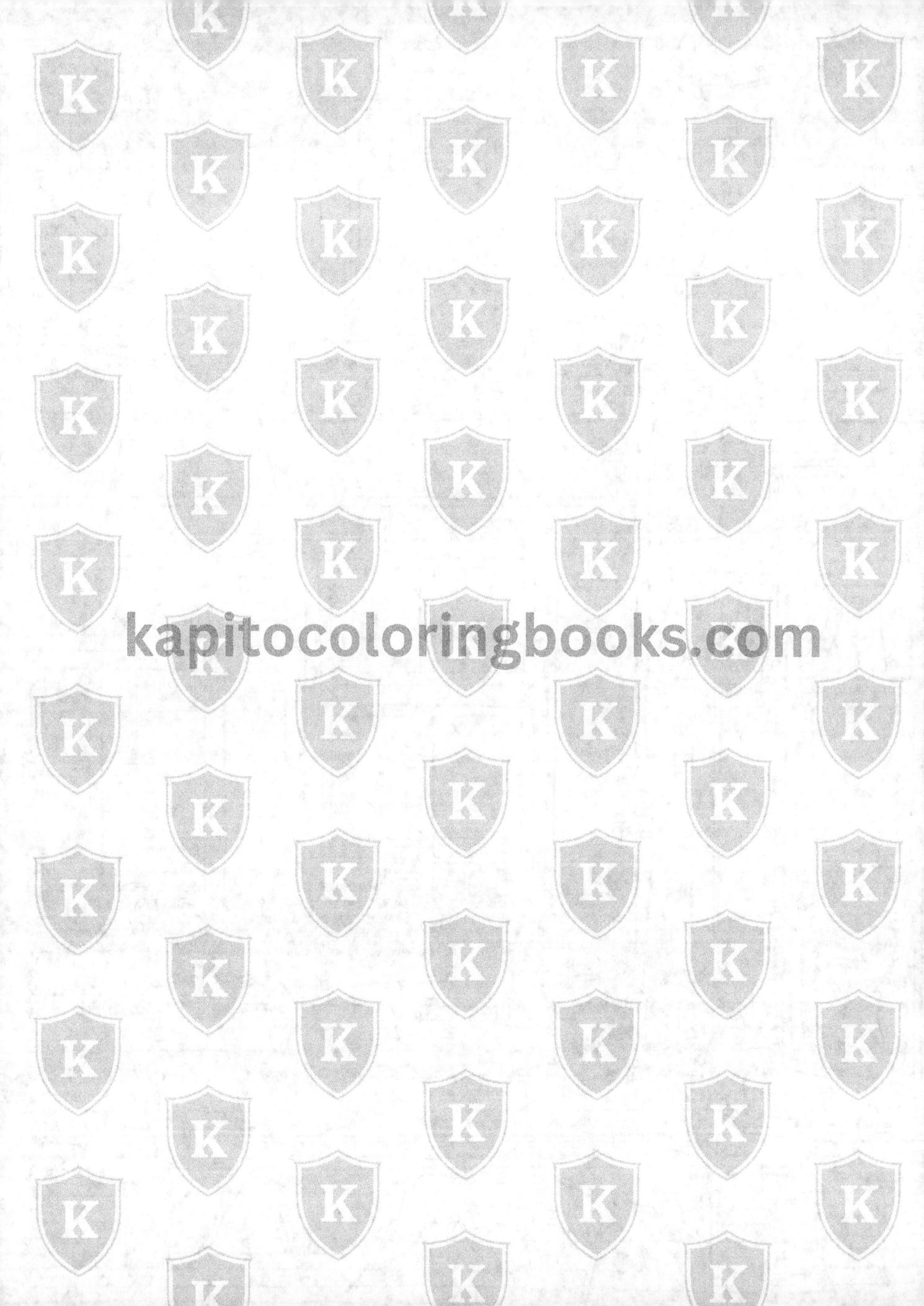

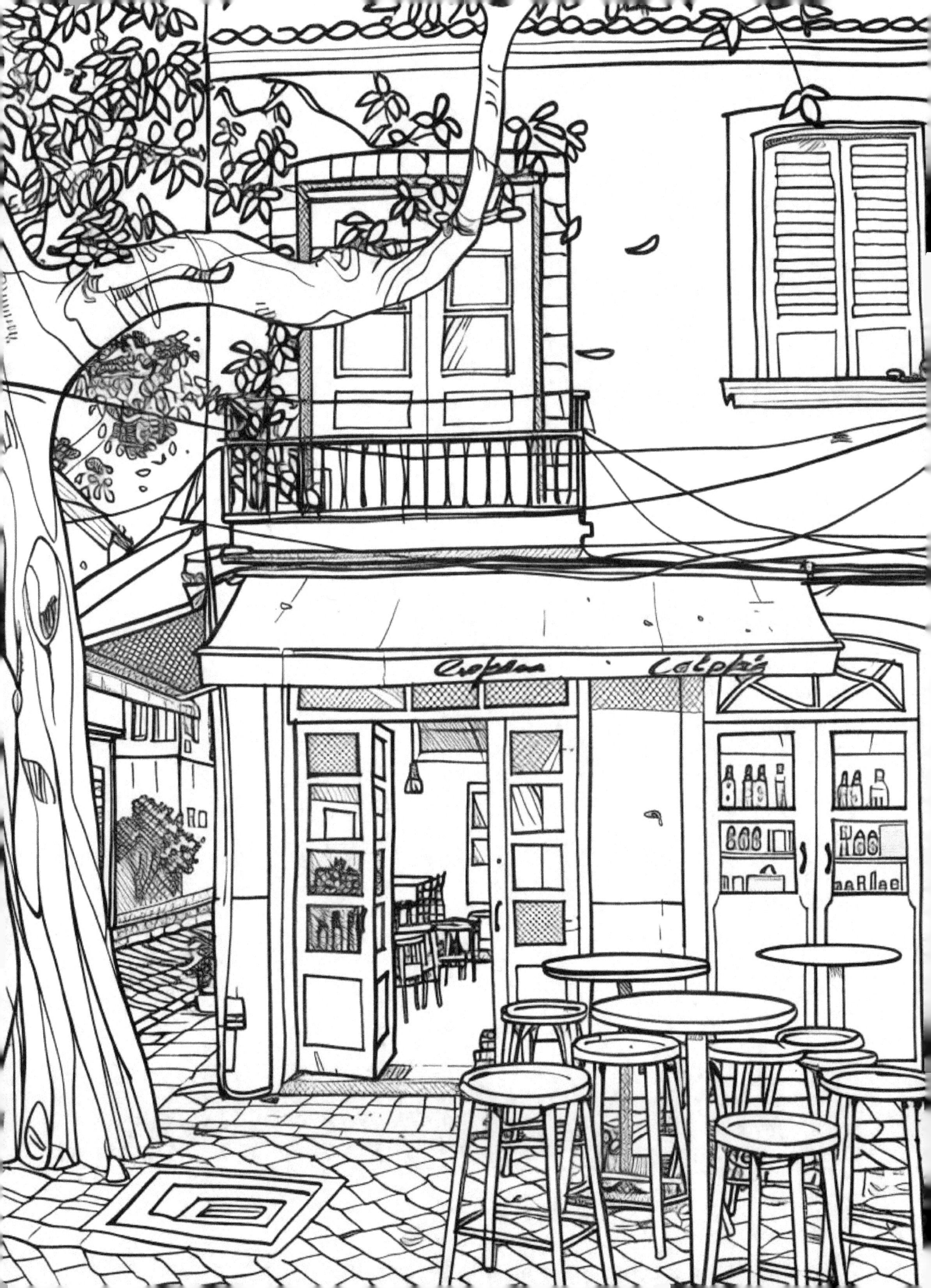

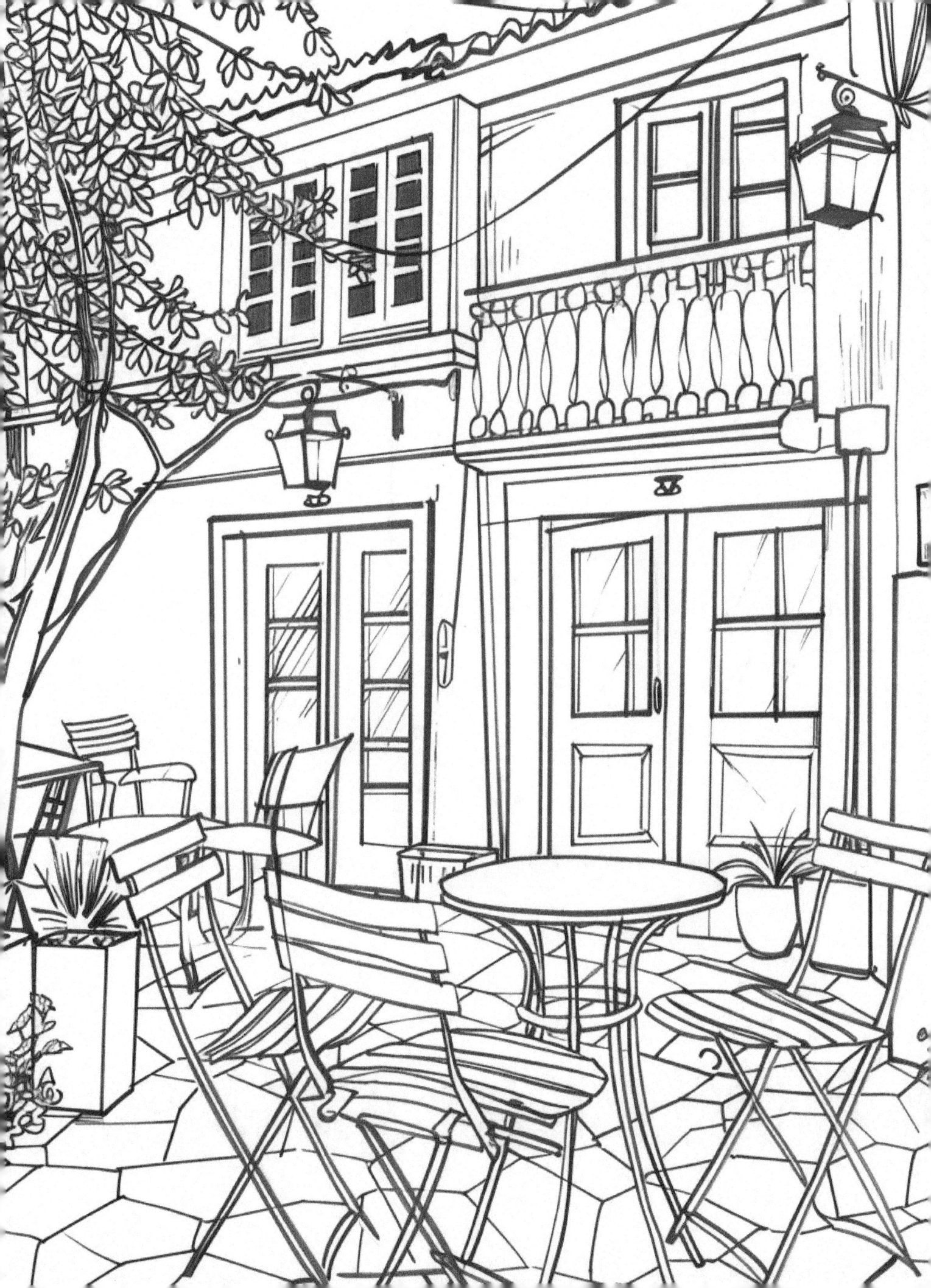

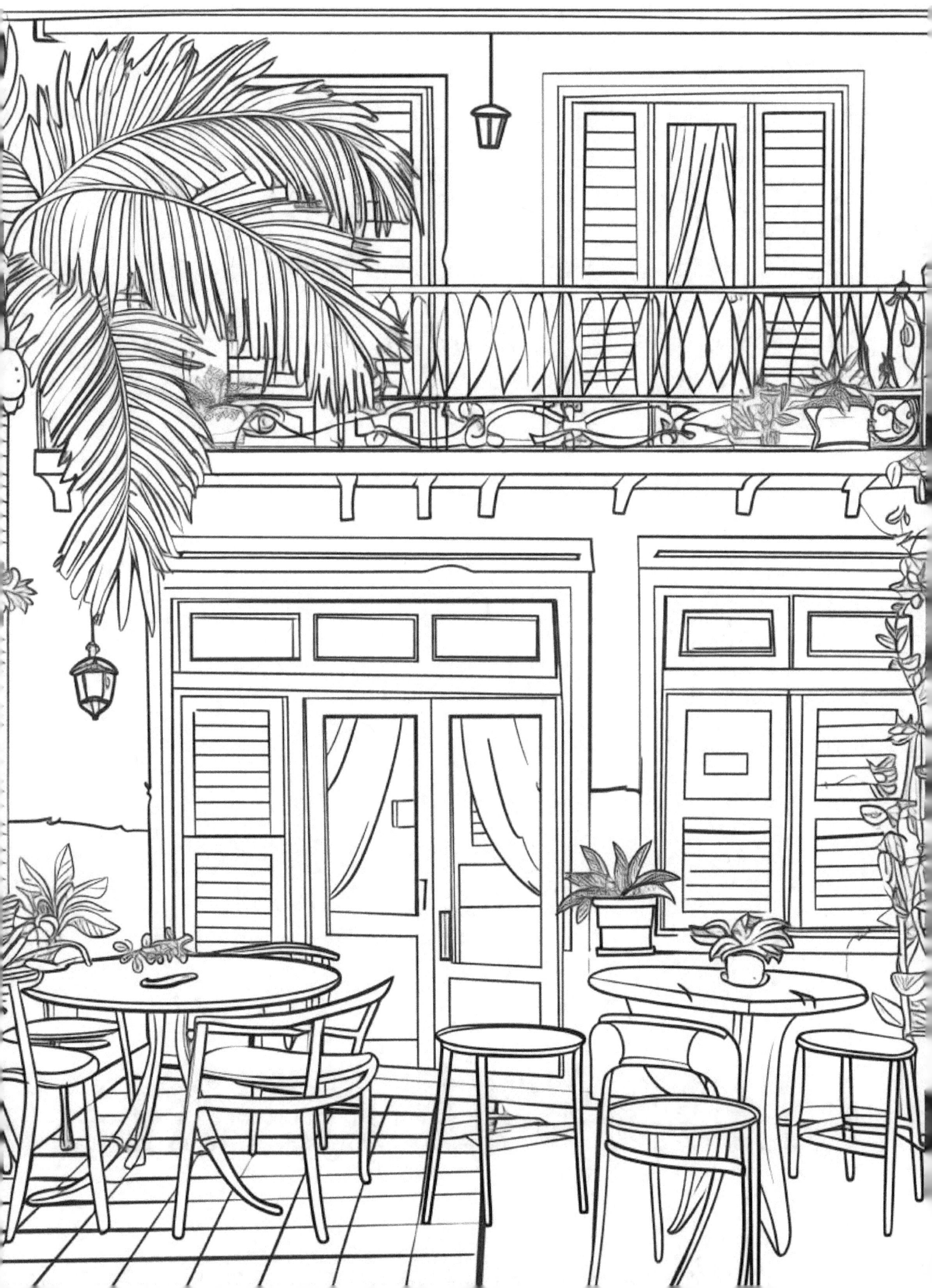

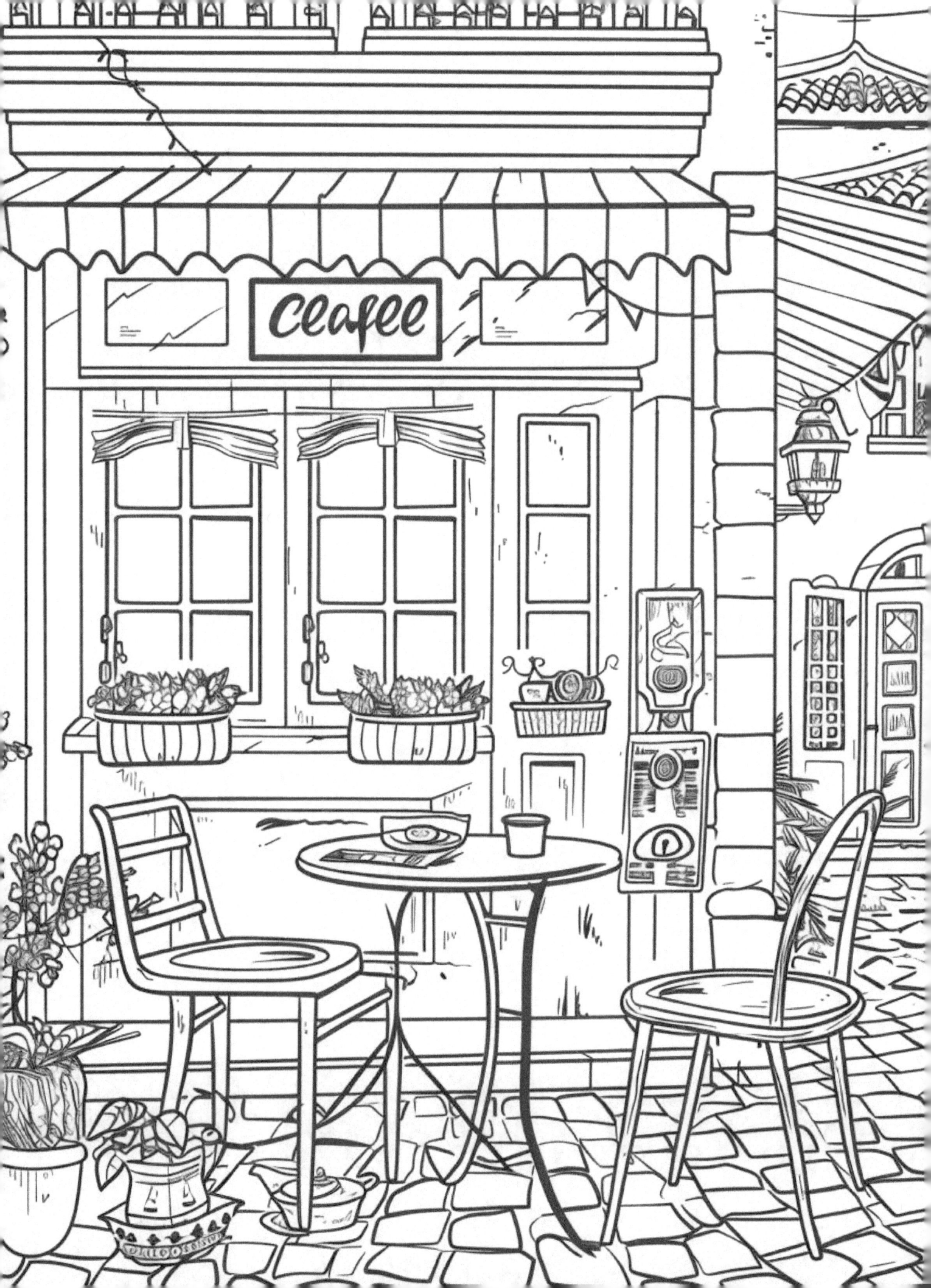

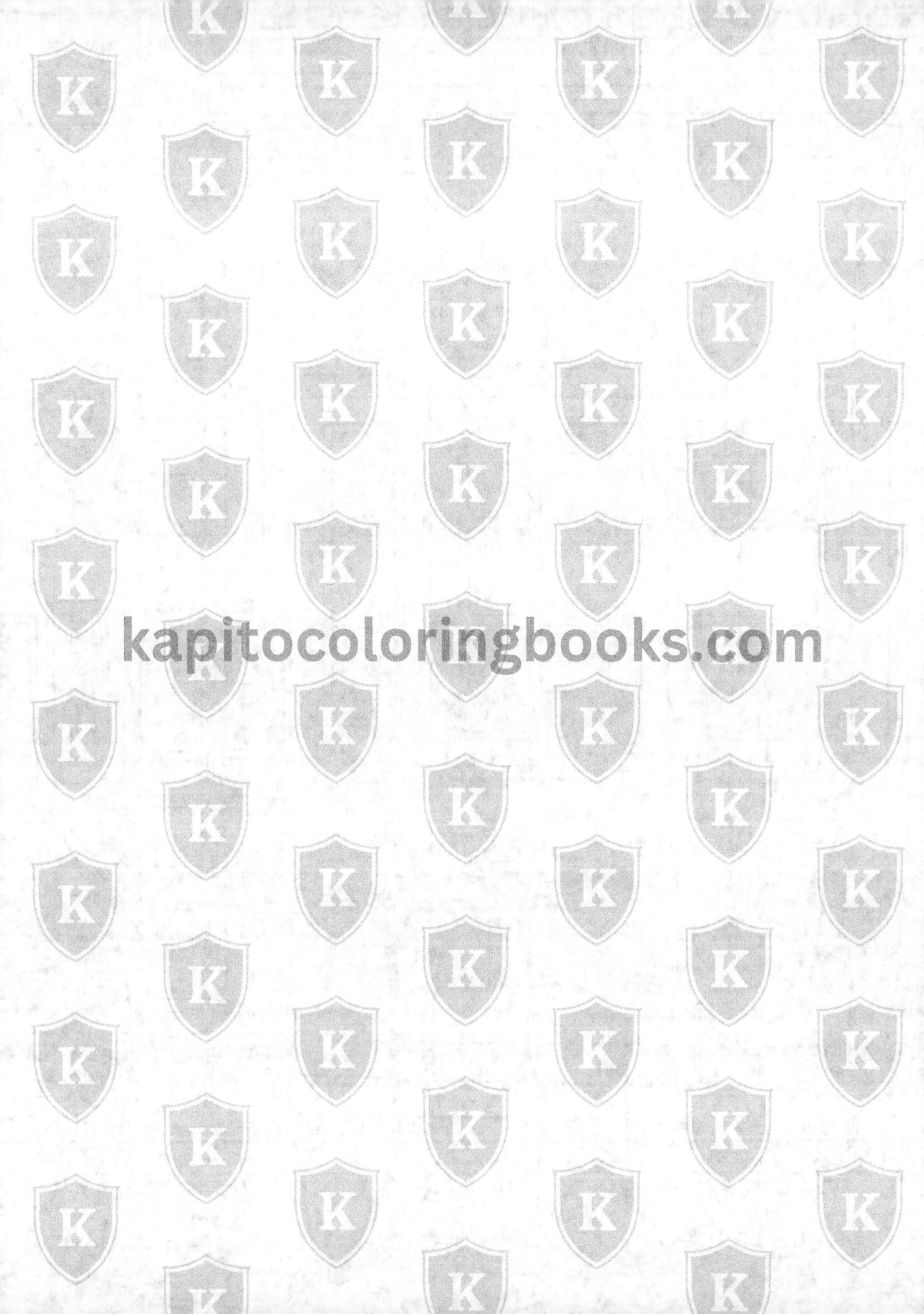

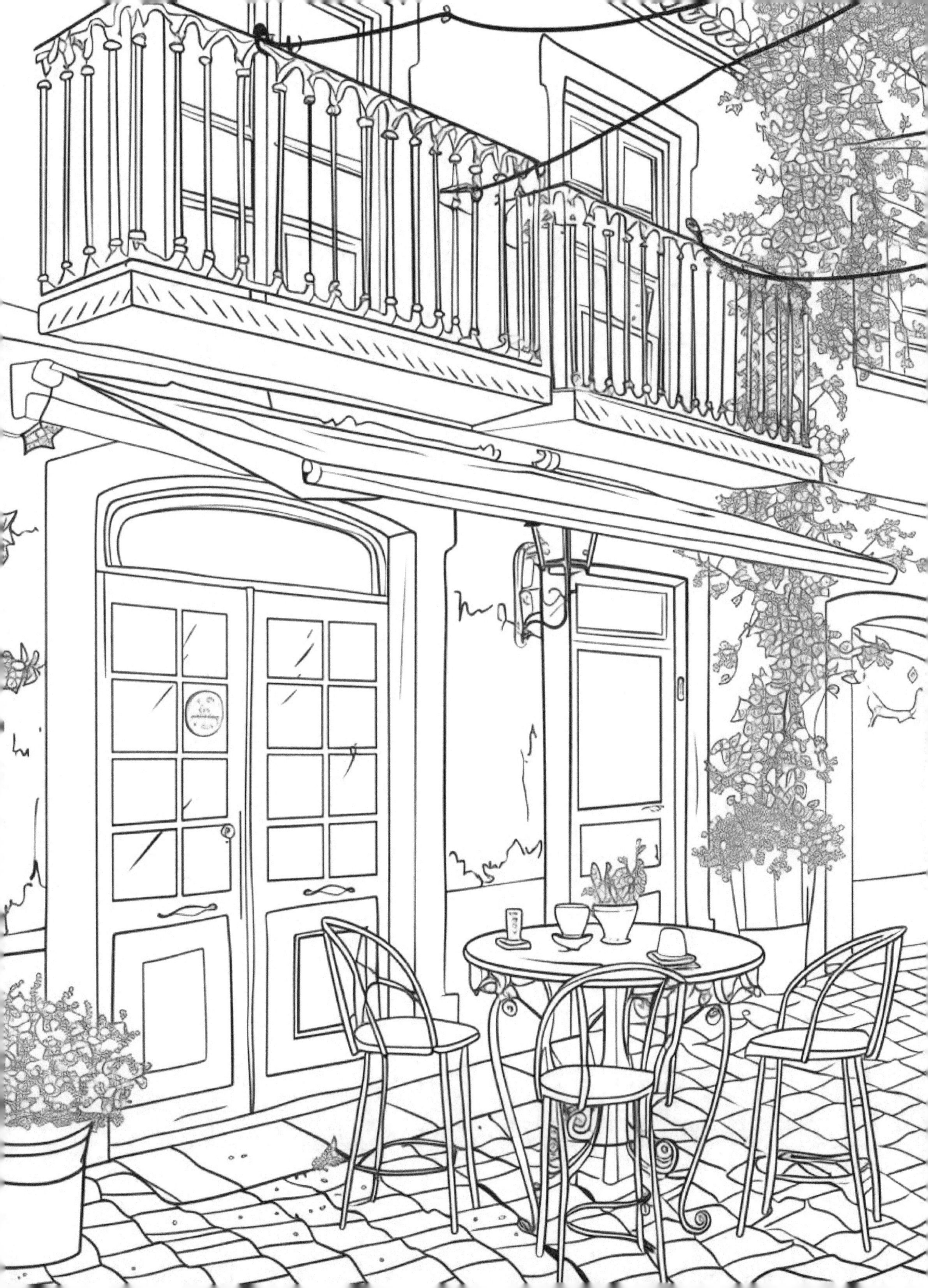

kapitocoloringbooks.com

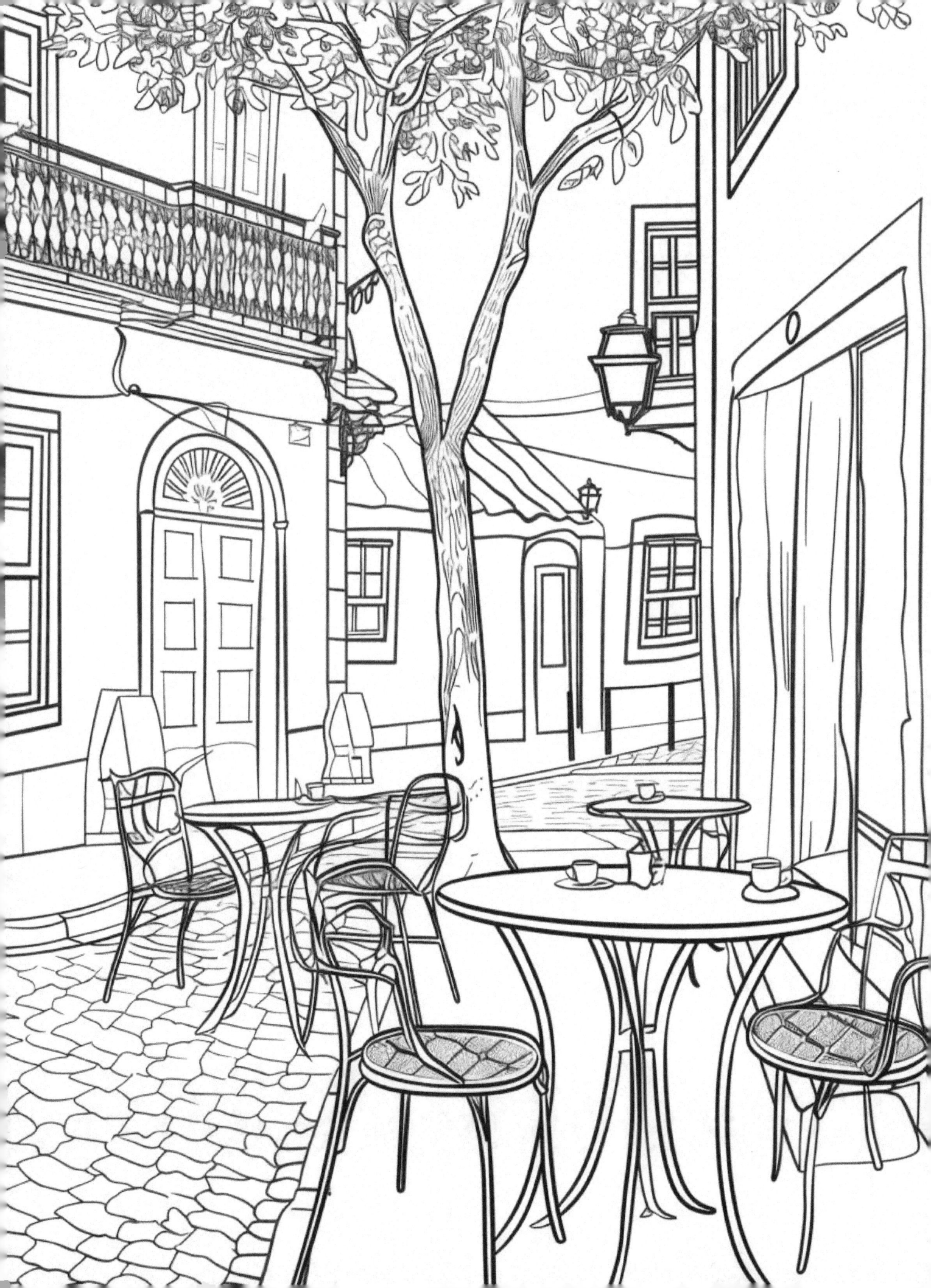

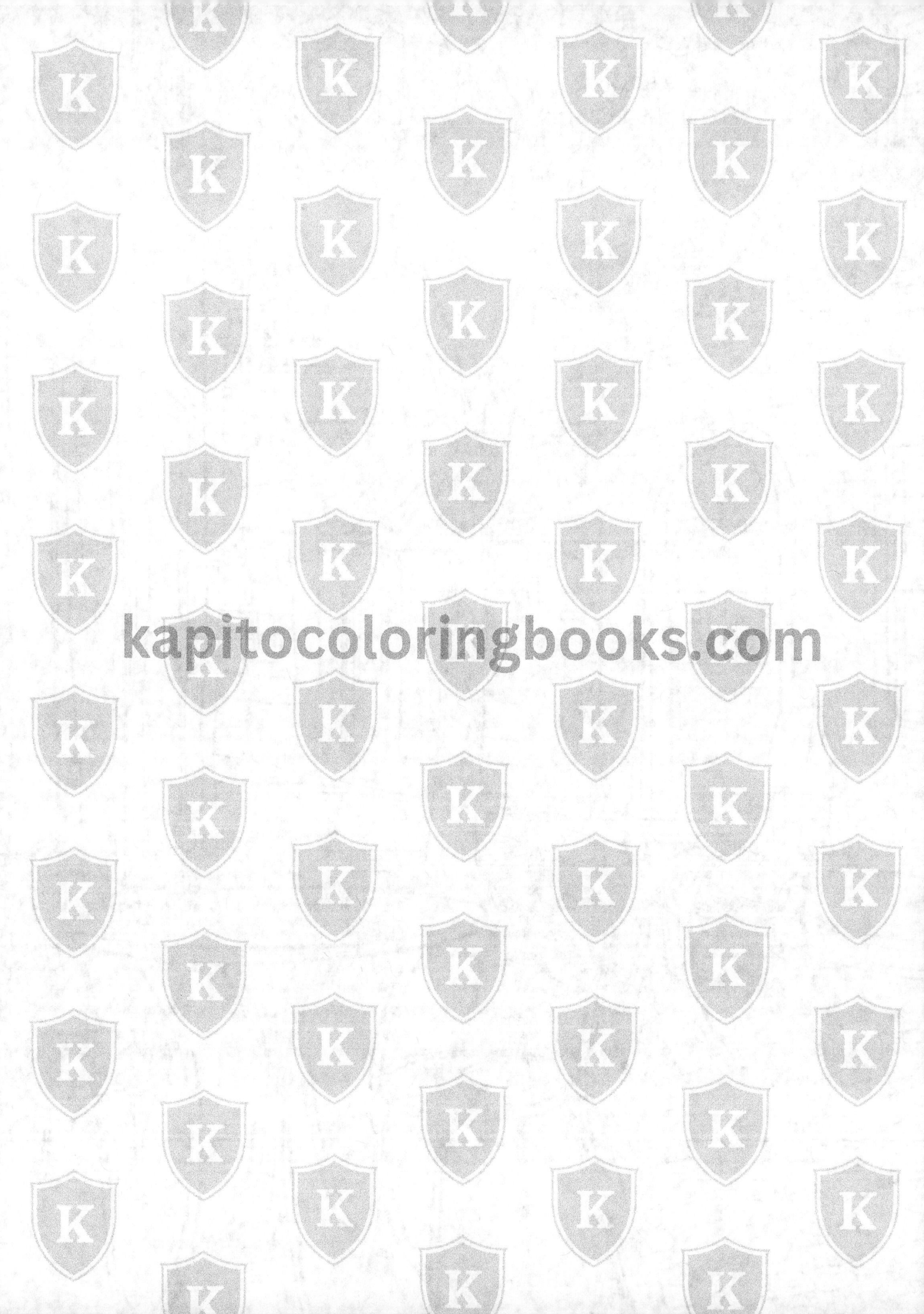

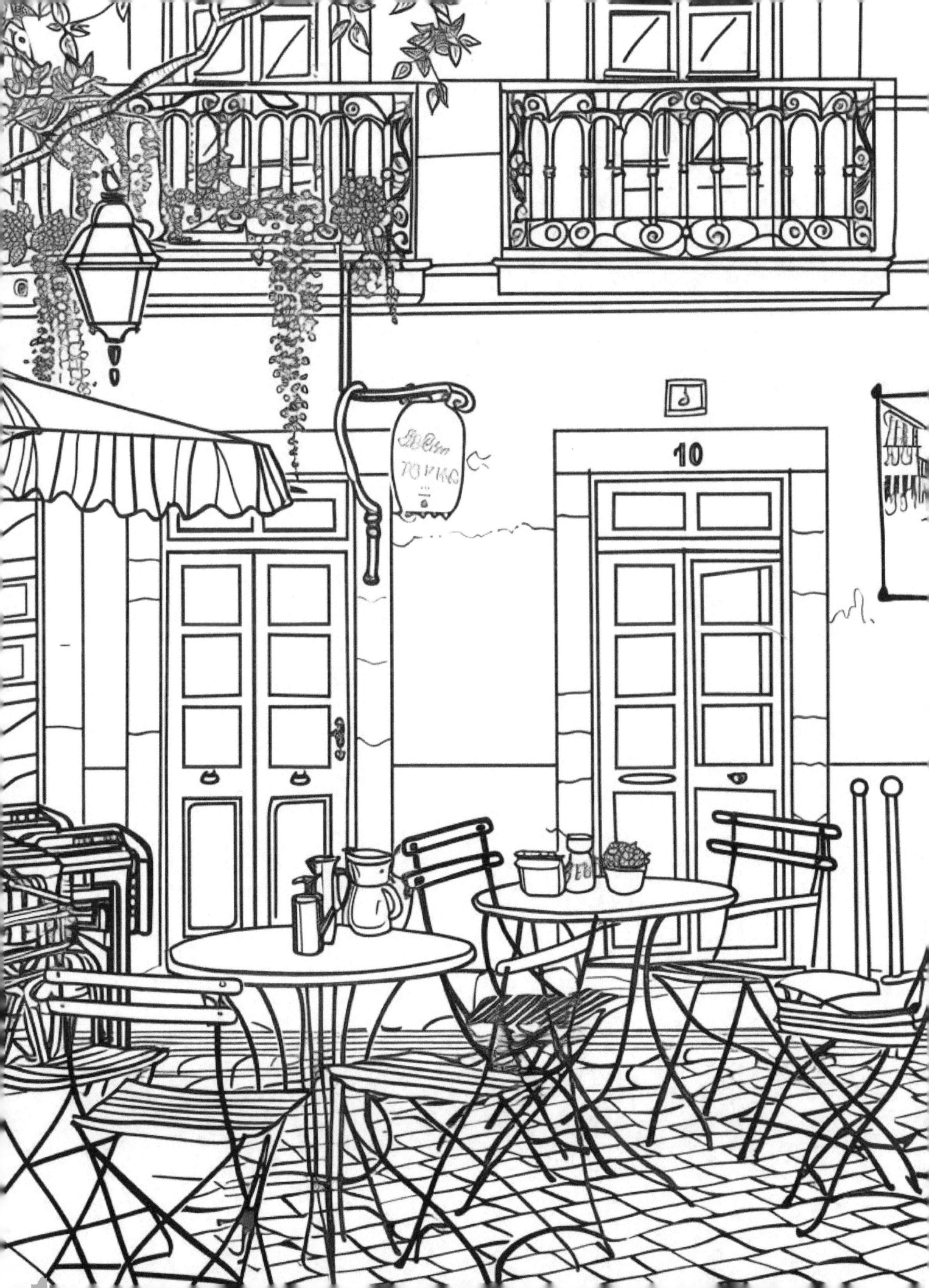

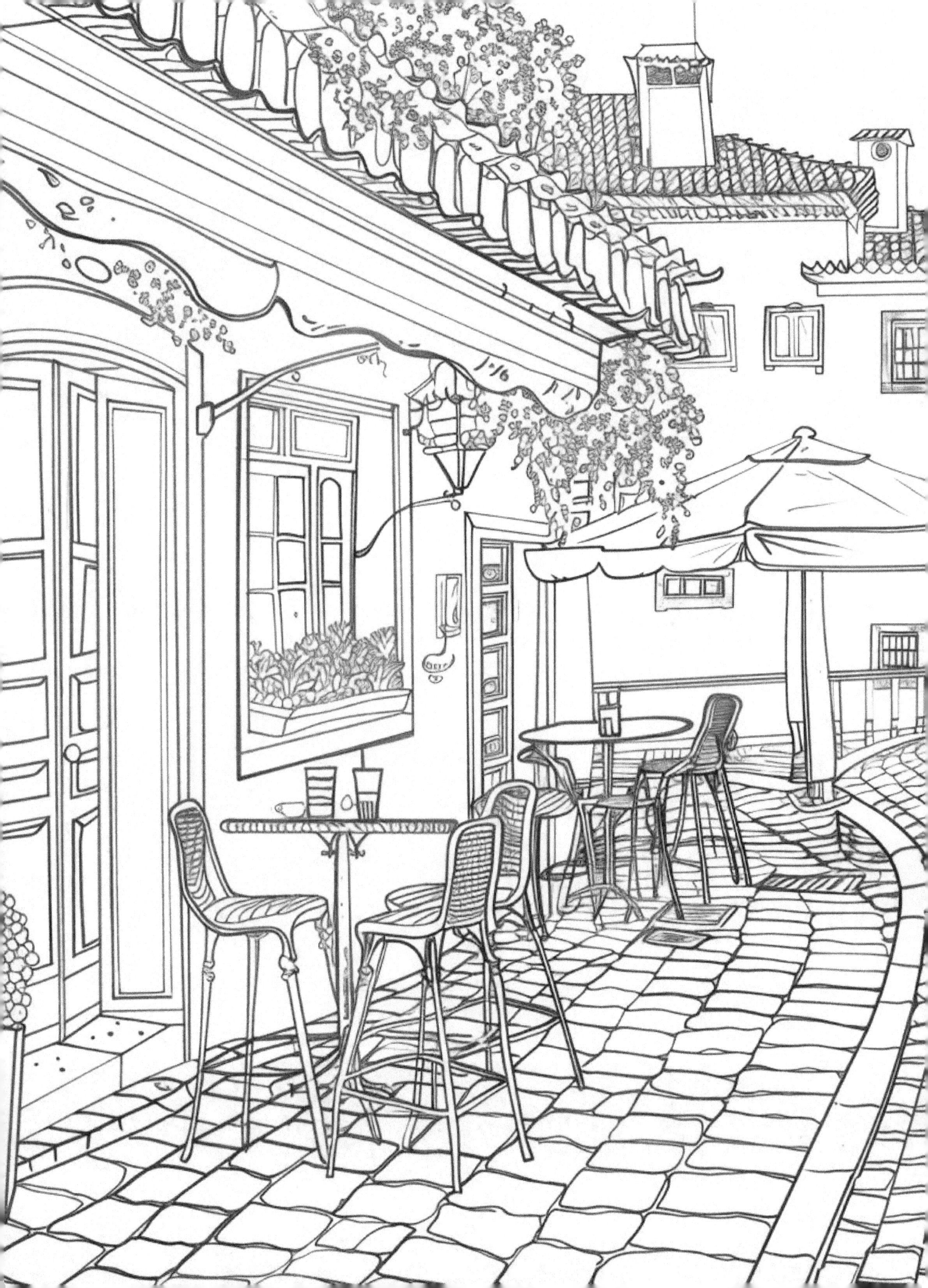

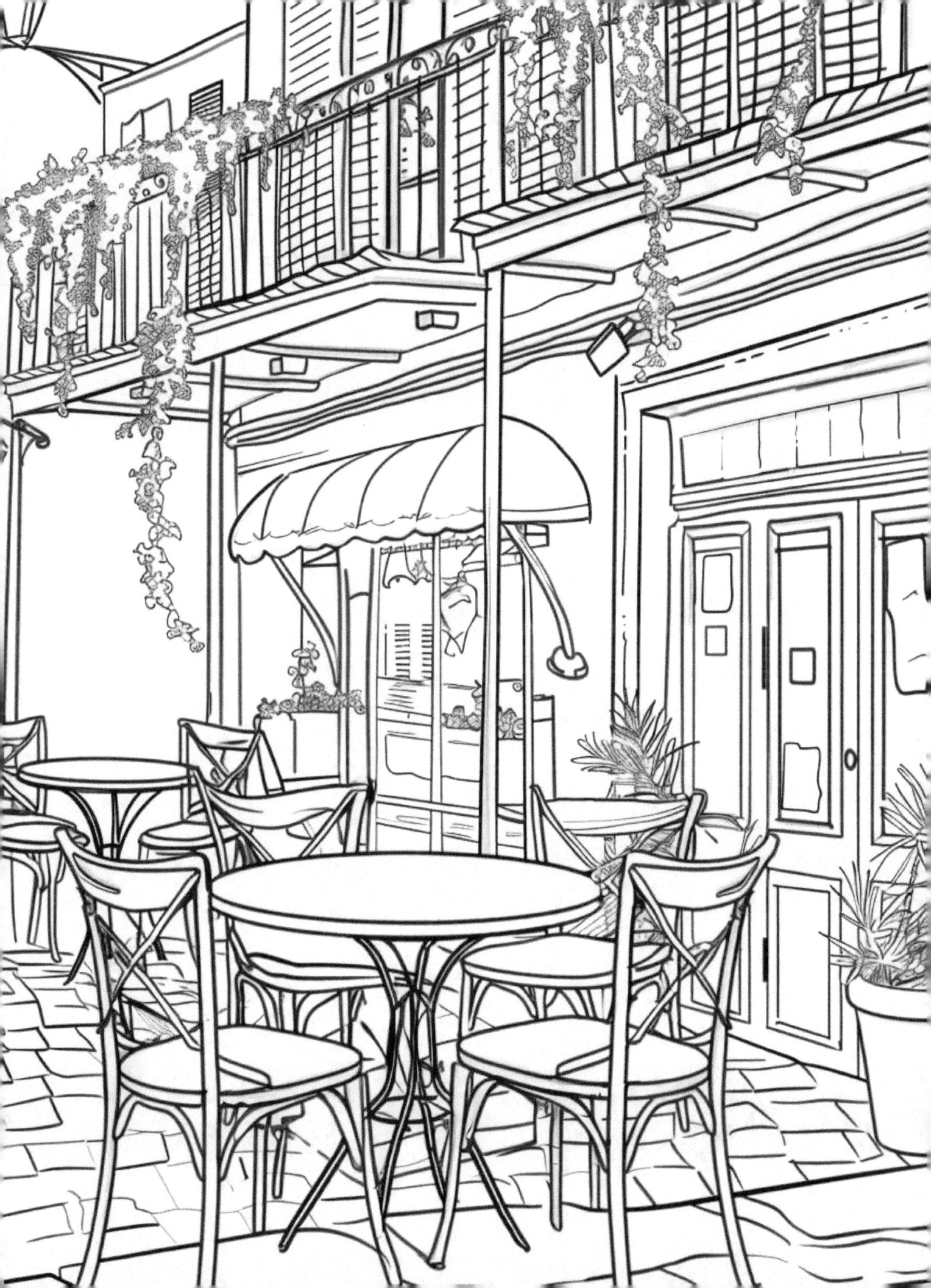

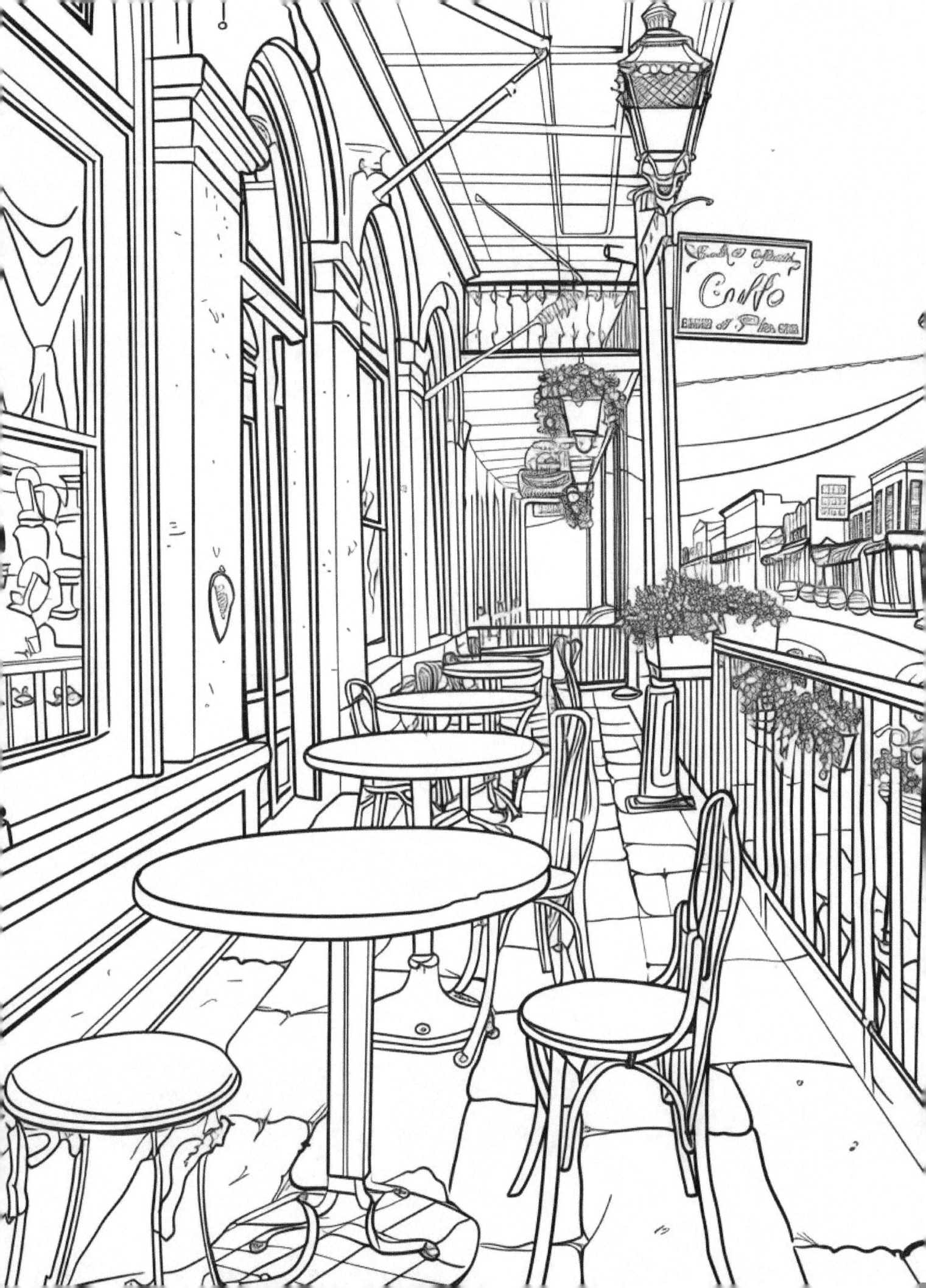

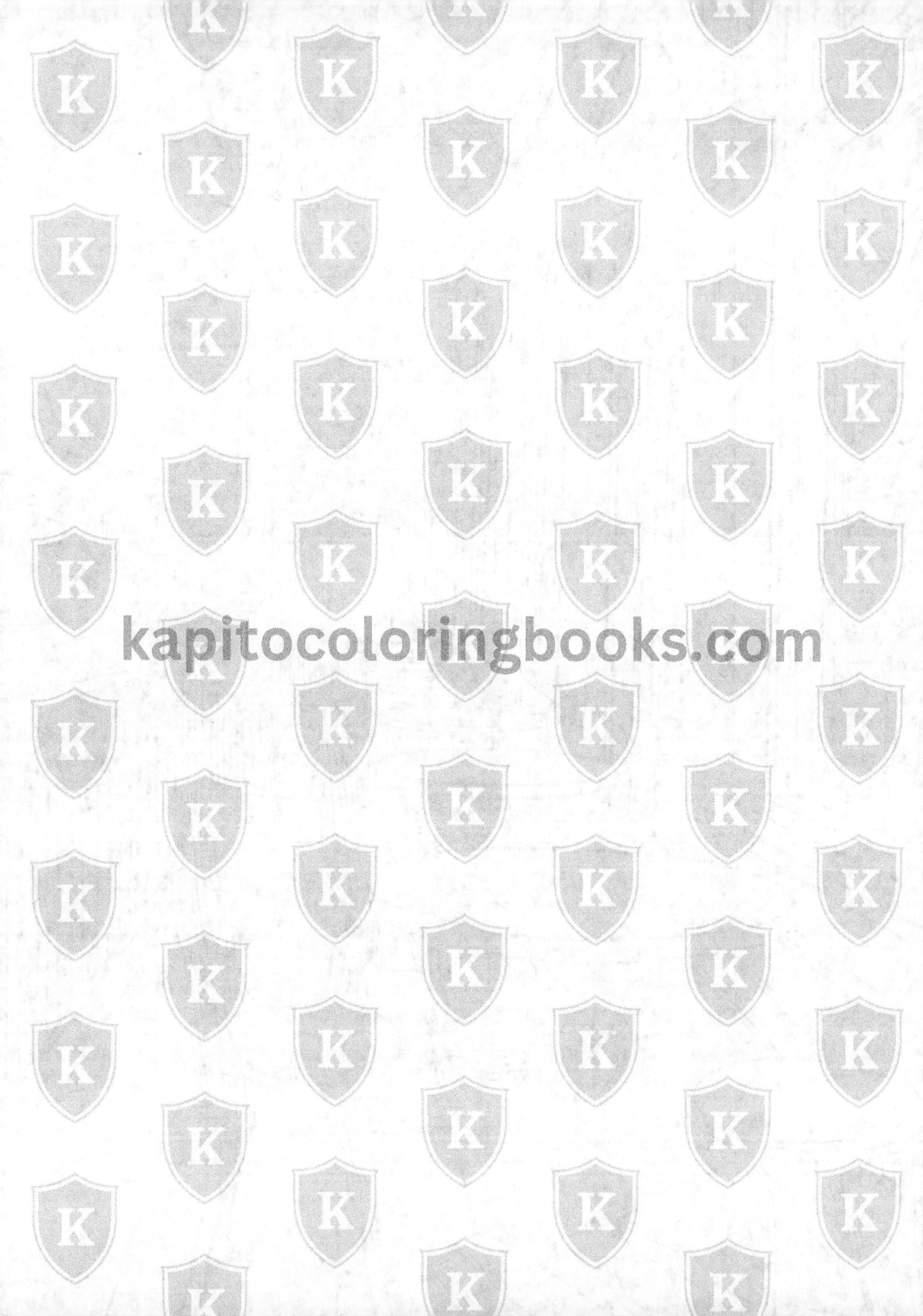
kapitocoloringbooks.com

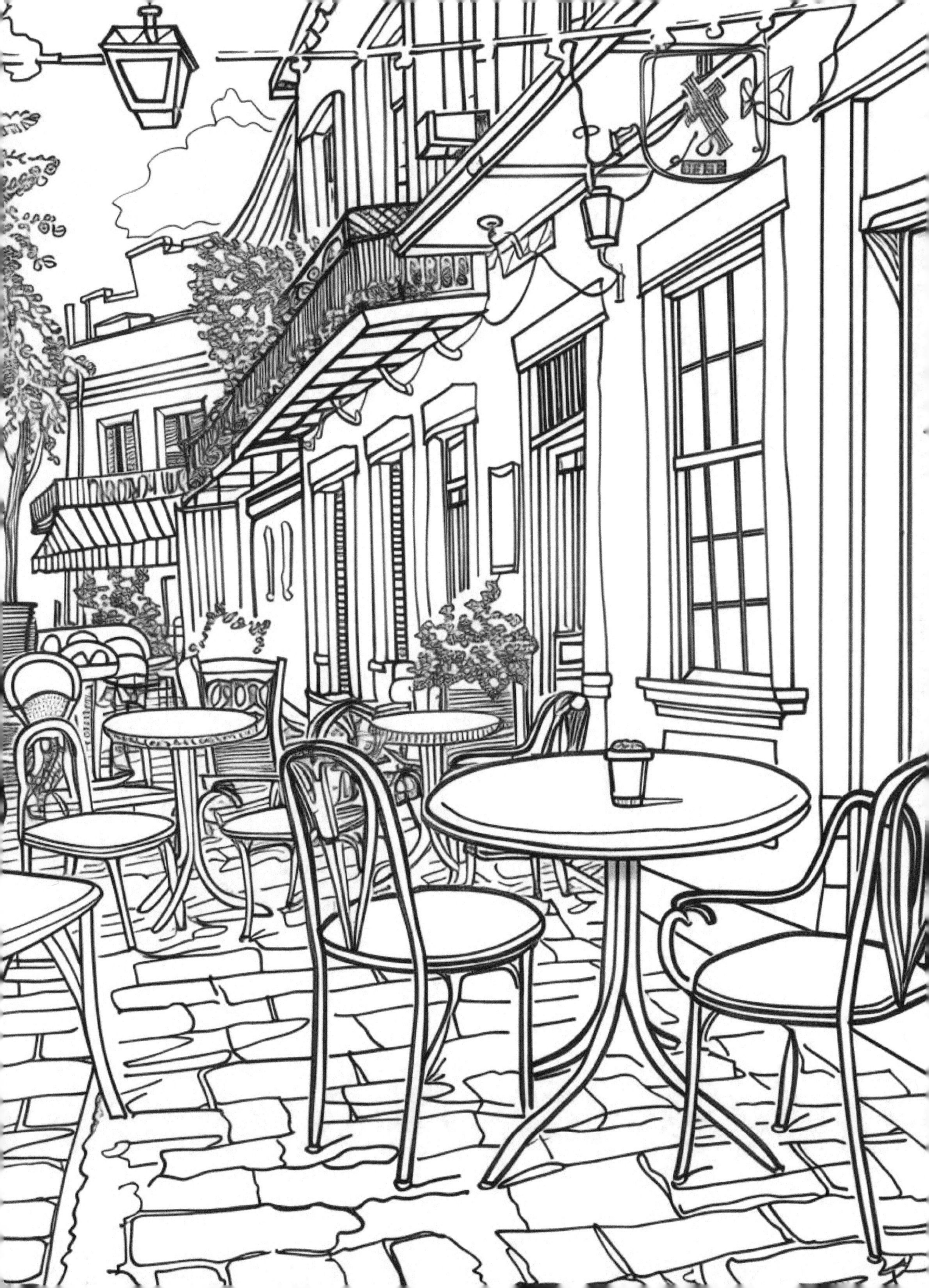

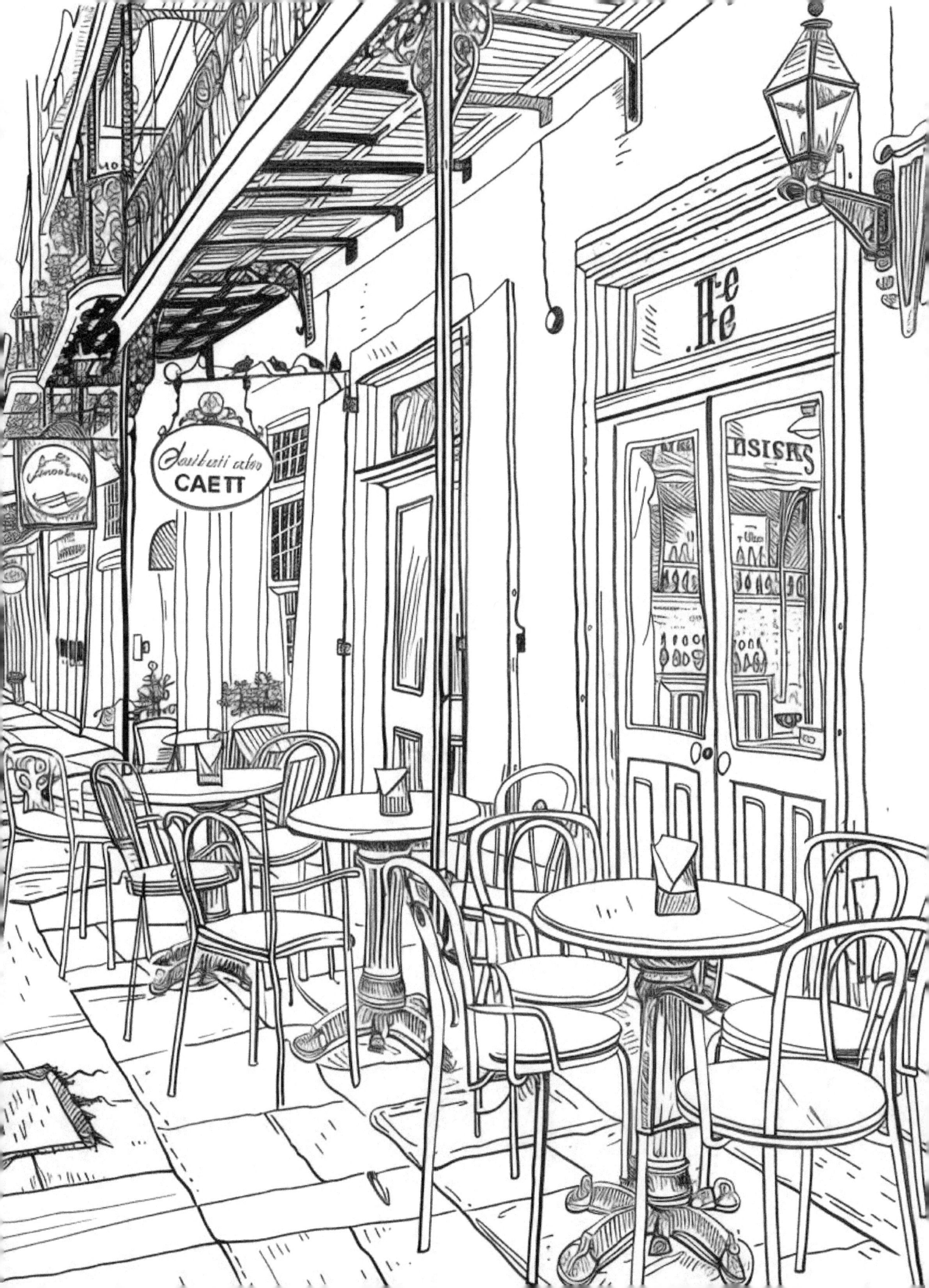

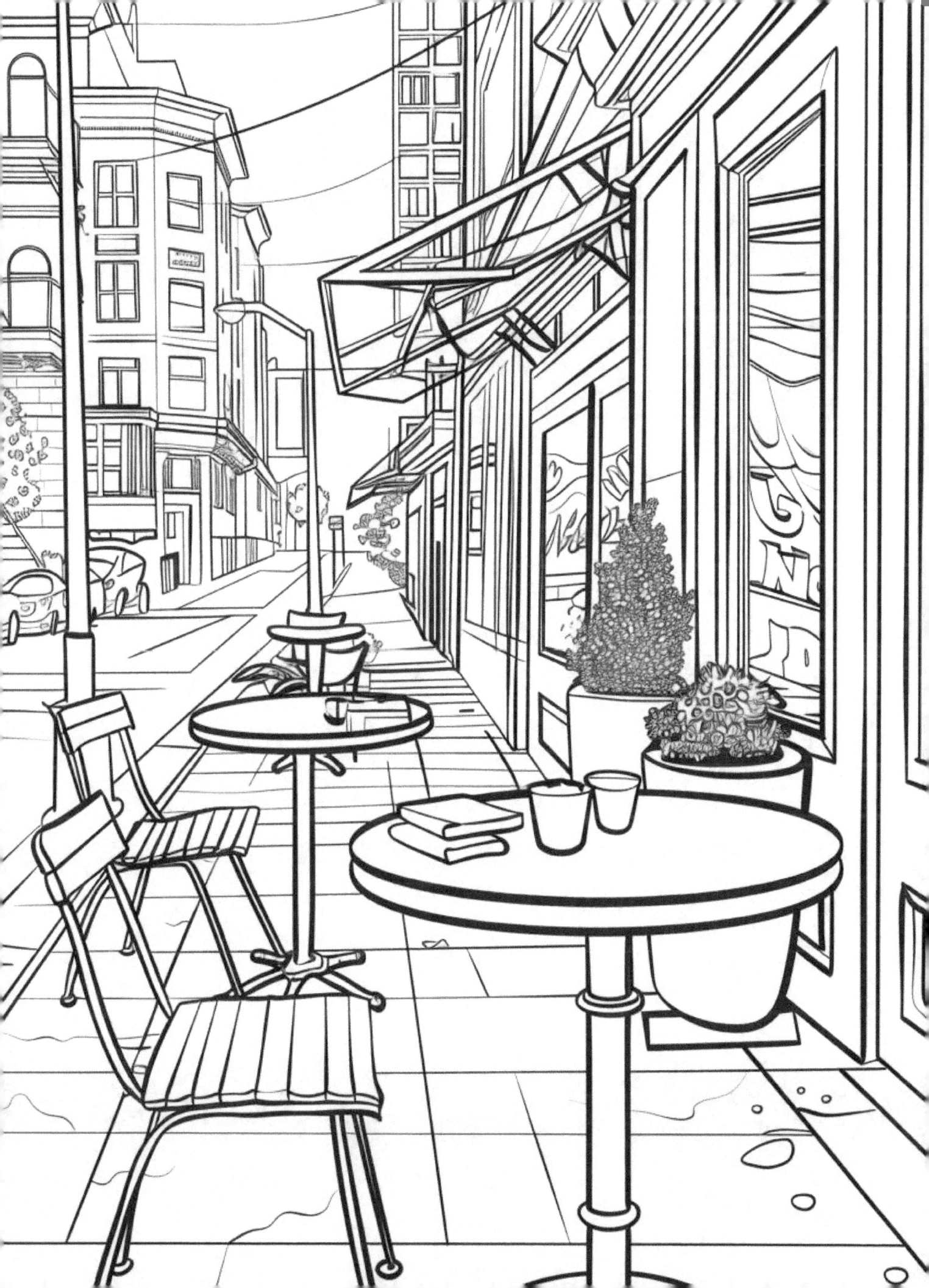

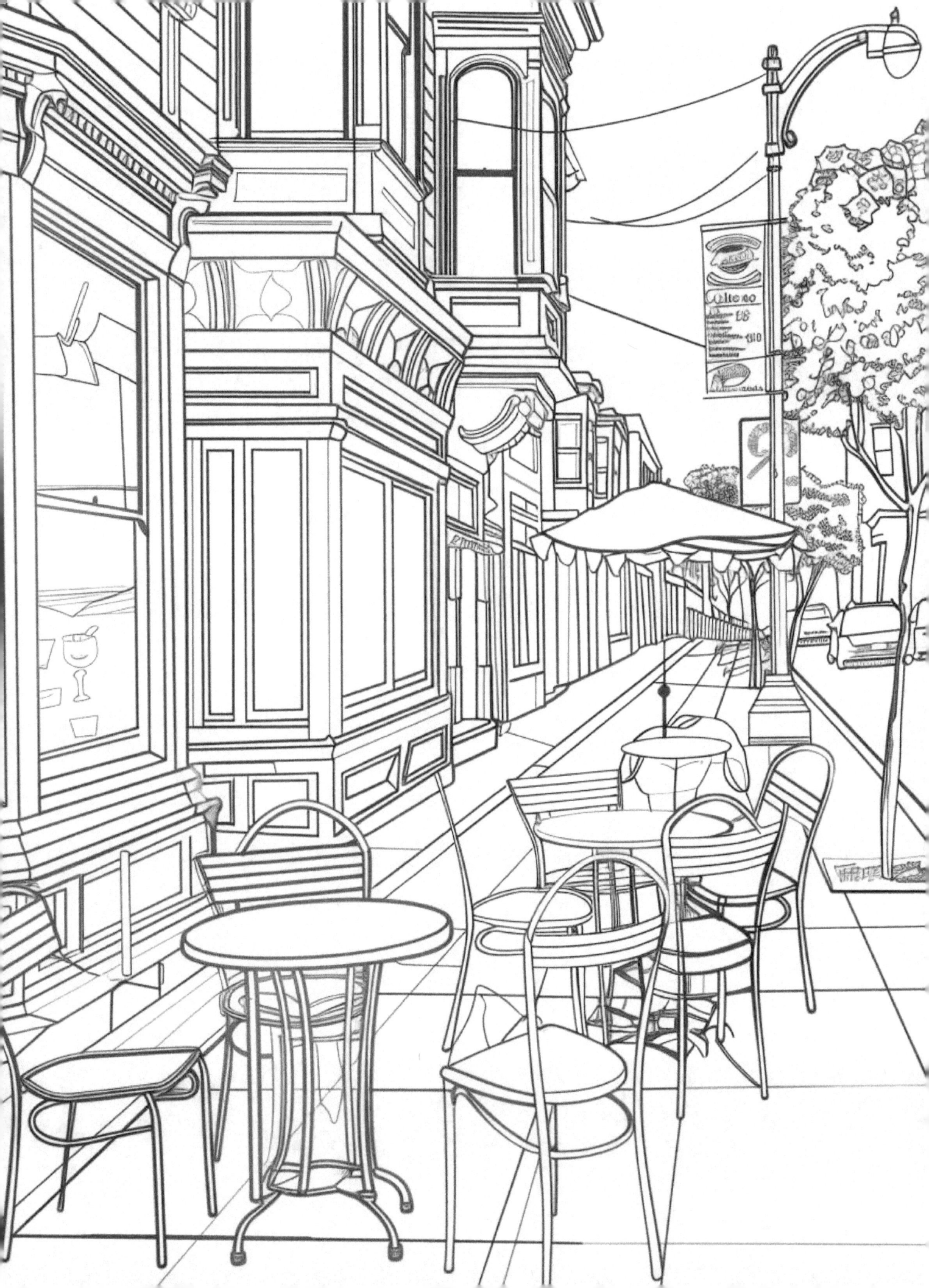

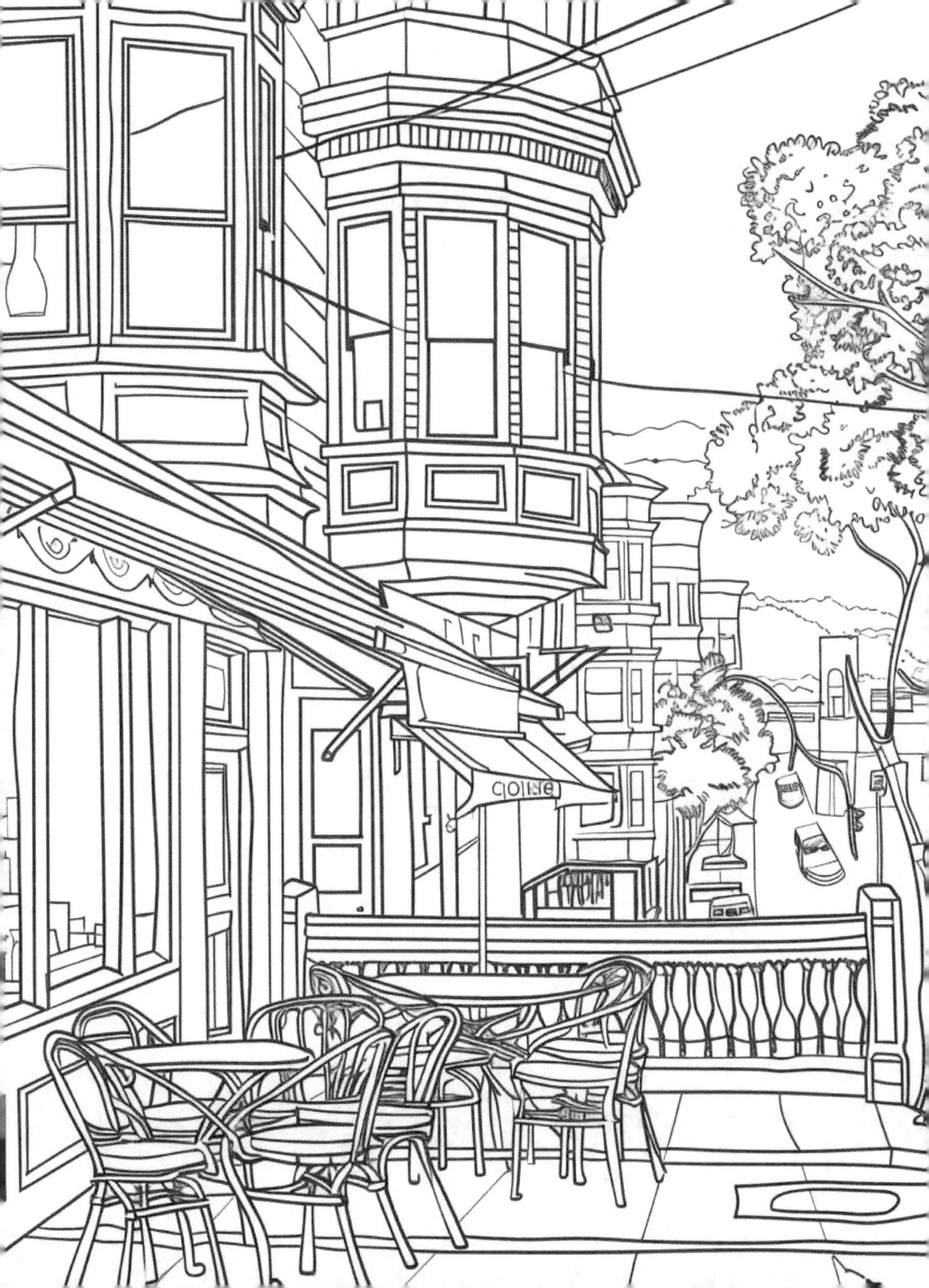

kapitocoloringbooks.com

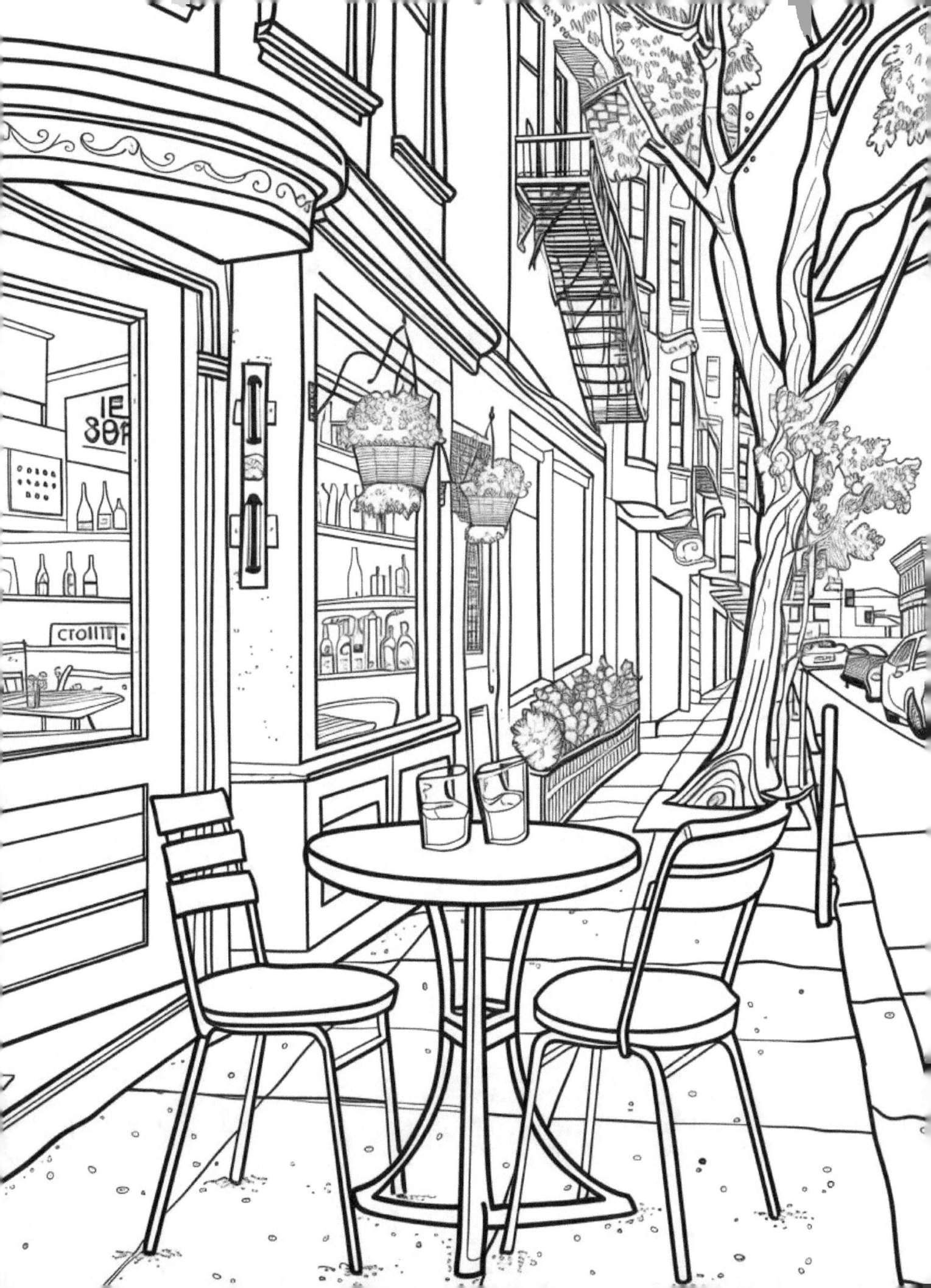

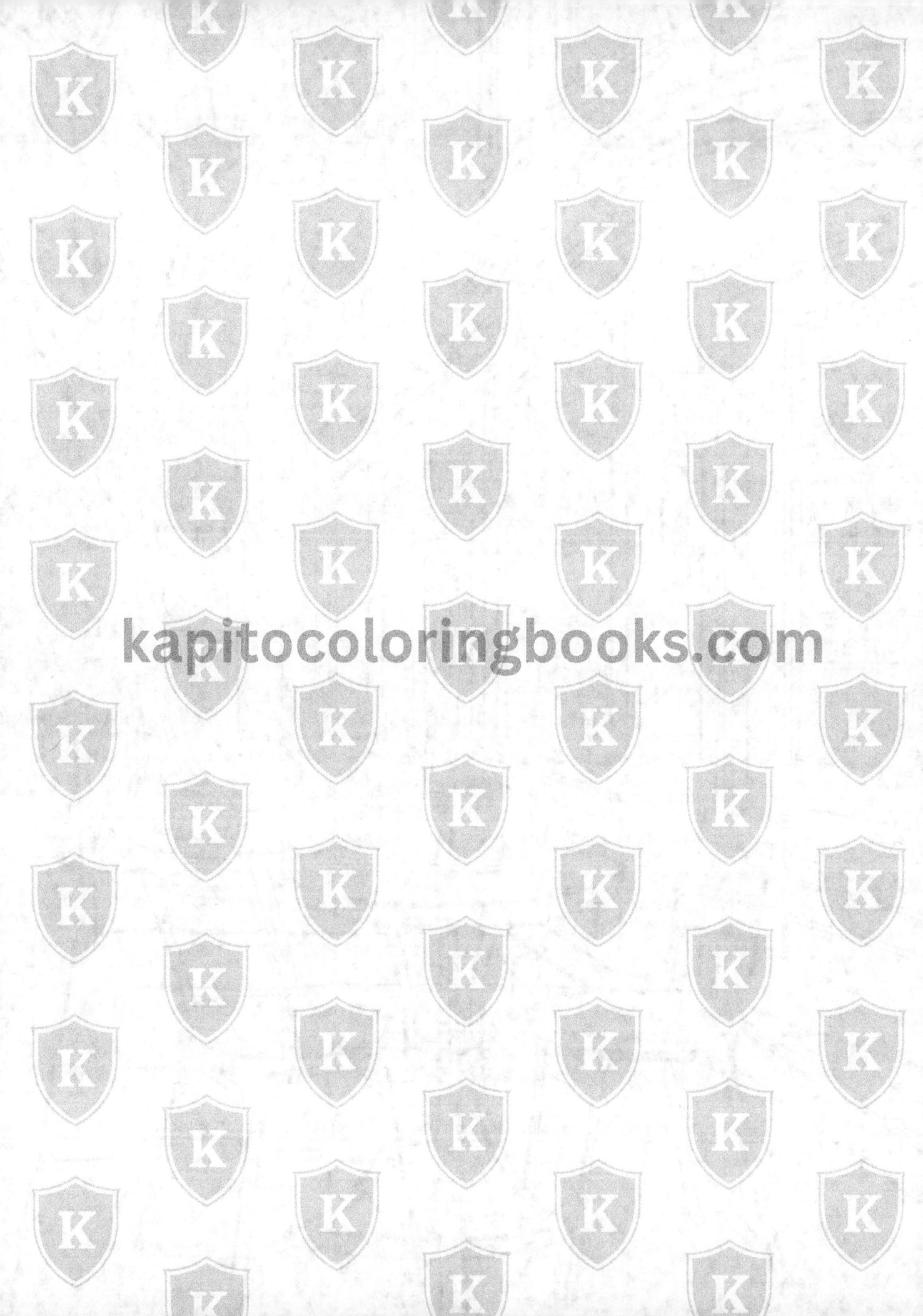